D1616164

THE
GERMAN
JETS IN ⊹
COMBAT

THE GERMAN JETS IN ✠ COMBAT

JEFFREY ETHELL & ALFRED PRICE

JANE'S
PUBLISHING COMPANY
LONDON · SYDNEY

First published in Great Britain by Jane's Publishing Company,
Macdonald and Jane's Publishing Group Limited,
Paulton House,
8 Shepherdess Walk,
London N1 7LW

ISBN 0 354 01252 5

Printed in Great Britain by
Purnell & Son Ltd, Paulton (Bristol) and London

Contents

Preface

Authors' Note

This book was conceived during an over-dinner chat with Bill Dean, who runs the Sky Books International bookshop in New York. After a discussion of aviation books in general, he was asked for his ideas on what might be a good seller in this line as a possible future work. 'Why not do something on the German jet aircraft?' he replied. 'There is a lot of interest in the subject and there must be a lot more to be said about them.' The conversation founded an idea, which led to a research project, which resulted in this book.

In collecting material for this work we have received generous assistance from several of those who flew the German jet aircraft and we should like to tender our grateful thanks to Guenther Wegmann, Rudolf Opitz, Horst Goetz, Hans-Georg Baetcher, Rudolf Schnoerrer, Walther Hagenah, Erich Sommer, Rudolf Zimmermann, Diether Lukesch, Peter Kappus and Rudolf Glogner. Several historians gave freely from their collections of material and photographs. In particular we should like to thank Arno Abendroth, who gave us tremendous help with the details of casualties to German pilots and jet aircraft losses. Also the authors would like to record their appreciation of assistance from Jay Spenser and Walter Boyne of the National Air and Space Museum at the Smithsonian Institution in Washington, Harold Watson, Richard Smith, Eddie Creek, Hanfried Schliephake, Hans Ring, Guenther Heise, Ken Bokleman and Bill Hess. David Irving kindly allowed us to quote a passage from his book 'The Rise and Fall of the Luftwaffe'. The authors also wish to acknowledge the valuable help received from the Public Record Office in London.

Jeffrey Ethell
Richmond,
Virginia,
USA

Alfred Price
Uppingham,
Rutland,
England

In this book German words have been anglicised where appropriate. Thus Günther has been written as Guenther, Köthen as Koethen and Böhlen as Boehlen.

Where measurements are given the metric figure is given first (kilometre, metre, kilogram) followed by the Imperial figure (mile, foot, pound). Where appropriate, conversion figures have been rounded out.

In writing this book the authors found great difficulty in marrying some of the British, American and German records concerning actions involving jet aircraft. Frequently the claims made by one side bear no relation in time or place to the losses admitted by the other. For this reason claims and losses have been linked in the text only where there is clear evidence for doing so; where there is no positive link, claims have in most cases been omitted.

Introduction

Although the ideas that spawned them were by no means new, it was not until the latter part of the 1930s that serious work began, initially in Germany, to develop gas turbines and rocket motors to power aircraft. Two factors spurred development work in these fields. First there was the general bid to improve the performance of military aircraft, as the nation strove to become the post powerful in Europe. And secondly there was the dawning realisation amongst aircraft designers that at speeds of over 720 kph (450 mph) the propeller-driven aircraft was fast approaching the limit of its performance capability; as speed increases the efficiency of the propeller as a means of converting rotational power into thrust falls rapidly, from around 80 per cent at 500 kph (310 mph) to only about 50 per cent at 1,000 kph (621 mph). In contrast the power from a gas turbine or rocket motor emerges as pure thrust so there are no such conversion losses; moreover in the case of the gas turbine the thrust actually increases with speed, due to the extra ram effect of the air entering the compressor.

For a major advance in any technical field three requirements have first to be met: first the 'background technology', the state of the art in metallurgy, machining and other related fields, must have reached the stage where it is possible to build it; secondly, some requirement for the advance must have been perceived by those with the power to switch resources to it; thirdly, and stemming from this, the necessary money and other resources must be available to bring the programme to fruition. By the end of the 1930s the means, the need and the money existed in Germany for the development of gas turbines and rocket motors for aircraft. This book tells the story of the three German jet aircraft which went into combat during the Second World War as a direct result of this pioneering work: the Messerschmitt Me 262, the Arado Ar 234 and the Messerschmitt Me 163.

Messerschmit

262

In the history of aviation few aircraft have been the subject of greater controversy than the Messerschmitt Me 262. Several commentators have drawn on its history to demonstrate the military ineptitude of Hitler and other German leaders who, it is said, failed to push its development with the necessary vigour or use the aircraft in the right way. Some have even gone so far as to suggest that, correctly used, the Me 262 might have changed the course of the Second World War. Such sweeping statements deserve careful analysis; and to provide that analysis we shall consider not only the technical development of the aircraft but also the military and political background to that development.

The Messerschmitt Me 262 stemmed from the firm's Project 1065, a design study to meet a 1938 requirement from the German Air Ministry, for a research aircraft powered by two of the new P 3302 gas turbine engines under development by the BMW Company. At the time the P 3302 was expected to develop a thrust of 600 kg (just over 1,300 pounds), and BMW confidentaly expected to have a pair of the new engines available for flight testing by the end of 1939. It proved to be a grossly over-optimistic prediction.

The airframe design produced by Dr Woldemar Voigt and his team was for a low wing monoplane with slight sweep-back on the wing, two jet engines and with the then-conventional tail wheel undercarriage. From the start the Messerschmitt team had tried to produce a design suitable for later development into an interceptor fighter, though the Luftwaffe requirement had not mentioned this. In March 1940 the company received a contract to build four examples of the new aircraft, which was now designated the Messerschmitt Me 262; three of the airframes were intended for flight testing and the fourth for static testing.

In the event BMW's timetable for its new engine proved to be wide off the mark. Not until the end of 1940, over a year late, was the first of these bench tested; and then it was found that it delivered a thrust of only 260 kg (570 pounds). In the meantime the Heinkel Company had pushed ahead with its own design for a gas turbine; on 27 August 1939, three days before the outbreak of the Second World War, one of these developing 500 kg (1,100 pounds) thrust had been the sole means

Opposite, top: **The third prototype Me 262, the first to get airborne on jet power alone, being readied for its maiden flight at Leipheim on 18 July 1942.** *Transit Films*

Centre: **Fritz Wendel boarding the aircraft.** *Transit Films*

Bottom: **The third prototype taking off.** *Transit Films*

The first prototype Messerschmitt 262 which, lacking the necessary jet engines, made its first flight powered by a Jumo 210 piston engine, from Augsburg on 18 April 1941 with Fritz Wendel at the controls. *via Schliephake*

of power for the specially-built Heinkel He 178 test aircraft.

As a result of the problems experienced by BMW with the novel form of power unit, the first Me 262 airframe was completed long before its engines. In order to test its handling characteristics, therefore, the prototype made its first flight on 18 April 1941 powered by a single nose-mounted Junkers Jumo 210 piston engine developing 690 hp. Test pilot Fritz Wendel took the aircraft on its maiden flight from the Messerschmitt airfield at Augsburg.

It was not until November 1941 that the first pair of flight-cleared BMW 003 engines (as the P 3302 was now known) arrived at Augsburg for installation in the Me 262. On 25 March 1942 Fritz Wendel took off in the new aircraft on the power of the Jumo piston engine and the two jet units; it was as well that the piston engine had been retained, for shortly after the take-off the jet engines failed one after the other and Wendel was only just able to get the badly underpowered aircraft back on to the runway.

It was now clear that the BMW 003 engine still required considerably more development work. So the Me 262 was modified to take the new Junkers Jumo 004 turbojet, which by the end of 1941 had completed its ten-hour running trial and was developing 1,000 kg (2,200 pounds) of thrust. On 18 July Fritz Wendel took off for the first Me 262 flight solely on jet power. The flight was normal apart from the

take-off: during the run, with the aircraft in the tail-down position, the elevators were blanketed by the wing and were ineffective; so when he reached flying speed Wendel had to touch his brakes to lift the tail off the ground, then the elevators functioned normally and he could get airborne.

Although the Me 262 soon demonstrated a maximum speed of around 800 kph (500 mph) and a climbing performance greatly superior to any other fighter in service, initially there was little Luftwaffe interest in the aircraft. In the summer of 1942 the Focke Wulf FW 190A and the Messerschmitt Bf 109G were equal or superior to anything in service with the Royal Air Force, the USAAF or the Soviet Air Force; Germany was not yet threatened with daylight bombing attacks and the main battle fronts were deep in the Soviet Union and in North Africa. At the primitive forward airfields an entirely new aircraft like the Me 262, with its short-lifed and unproven jet engines which required careful handling and skilled maintenance, would have been of little value. The need was for ever-greater numbers of conventional fighters for the final push to victory, rather than such a temperamental novelty even if it did have a far higher performance. Nevertheless, to keep abreast of the new technology, in May 1942 the Luftwaffe placed an initial order for 15 pre-production Me 262 fighters; in the following October this was increased to thirty. The development of the new fighter was to be pushed ahead to the point where it could be placed into full production, if required.

The mood in the spring of 1943 may be gauged from part of the minutes of the produc-tion conference held in Berlin on 31 March, with *Generalfeldmarschall* Erhard Milch in the chair. The Messerschmitt Me 209, a linear development of the 109, was discussed; if the Me 262 was to be placed in large-scale production, it would have to be at the expense of the Me 209. Milch commented: 'Dinort (*Oberst* Oskar Dinort, one of Milch's staff officers) has proposed that the Me 209 should be dropped and everything concentrated on the 262. We have discussed the matter, and I consider such a move premature.' *Generalmajor* Adolf Galland, the inspector of fighters, agreed with him: 'We should not do it.' The Me 209 was to be hastened into production with all possible speed; the Me 262 could replace it in production later — if the war lasted that long.

During the weeks that followed, however, there was a considerable shift of opinion in favour of the Me 262. In May Adolf Galland visited Lechfeld and flew the fourth prototype; he was so impressed that on his return to Berlin he urged that the jet fighter be placed in production as soon as possible, and receive priority over all others. Milch accepted Galland's recommendations; the Me 209 was to be dropped from the production schedule. A few days later, on 28 May, came further pressure to push ahead with the Me 262. Engineer *Oberst* Dietrich Schwenke, head of the department responsible for assessing the latest enemy equipment, informed a meeting in Berlin that a talkative RAF prisoner had let slip that during a visit to Farnborough the previous Christmas he had seen '... a propellerless aircraft flying at an altitude of 300 m (about 1,000 feet) and in his opinion it was very fast. This is the first

mention of an enemy jet fighter ...' *General-major* Wolfgang Vorwald, head of Milch's technical department, commented that such a development by the enemy was certainly possible.* It seemed to be an ominous pointer to the future; and for the present things were gradually becoming more and more difficult for the Luftwaffe, as the latest British, American and Soviet fighters proved uncomfortably equal to the best machines the Luftwaffe had in service. Now it was clear that only the Me 262 could provide the jump in performance necessary to overcome the numerical advantage likely soon to be enjoyed by the enemy fighter forces.

At a production conference held in Berlin on 29 June, attended by Willi Messerschmitt, Milch was informed of the current position regarding the planned production of the Me 262:

'Construction of the wings, and final assembly, will take place at Augsburg and construction of the fuselages and tails will take place at Regensburg. By concentrating our effort and if certain suppositions are realised, we can have delivery of the first production aircraft by January 1944. Production will then rise in the second month to 8, in the third to 21, in April to 40 and in May to 60 aircraft. By the middle of May we shall reach the requested number of 100 aircraft and production will run at 60 per month until November ...'

This was a poor time to play politics with the equipment for the Luftwaffe, but this is what now happened. And the culprit was Willi Messerschmitt. Piqued at the rejection of his firm's Me 209, he now resolved to keep it in production *with* the Me 262 and tried to increase his pool of skilled manpower to bring this about. An inveterate empire-builder, Messerschmitt was able to pull sufficient strings with Nazi party officials to retain the Me 209 in the production schedule for several months after Galland and other senior Luftwaffe officers had said it was no longer needed. But the additional skilled workers necessary to tool up two aircraft production lines instead of one were not forthcoming, with resultant delays to both programmes. Not until November 1943 was the Me 209 finally dropped from production, and the Messerschmitt Company's efforts concentrated on the Me 262.

In the meantime the test programme of the Me 262 was gathering momentum. In July the fifth prototype, the first to be fitted with a tricycle undercarriage albeit a fixed one, made its first flight. It was followed in November by the sixth prototype, the first pre-production machine with a retractable tricycle undercarriage and slightly revised engine nacelles.

Up till now the Messerschmitt Me 262 had been considered solely as a bomber destroyer. But like other fighters in production for the Luftwaffe (and, indeed, those of other air forces), it was planned that the aircraft should be able to carry bombs and be used in the secondary role of fighter-bomber. In view of the frequency with which the story of the Me 262 in the fighter-bomber role has been misrep-

*The machine referred to was the Gloster E 28/39, the first British jet propelled aircraft, one example of which was flying in the winter of 1942.

resented, it is important to examine it now in some detail.

During the great air battles fought over Germany in the summer and autumn of 1943 the defences had aquitted themselves well. The available bomber-destroyers, and in particular the heavily armed Messerschmitt 110s and 410s, had demonstrated that they could inflict swingeing losses on the unescorted US heavy bomber formations. At the time it seemed to many Luftwaffe leaders that, given an increase in the number of conventional bomber-destroyers, the threat of the daylight attacks could be erased altogether.

Meanwhile, there could be no doubting that the Western Allies were making intensive preparations for a major invasion operation to be launched the following year, somewhere in north-western Europe. Hitler saw clearly that the battle to secure the beachhead would be decisive to the course of the war: if the German forces could beat off the invasion, the Allied losses would almost certainly be so great as to preclude another attempt for one or perhaps even two years; and in the meantime powerful forces could be released for the Eastern Front. But if the defensive battle was lost and the Allied forces were able to establish themselves ashore, Germany would be squeezed between the eastern and western fronts like a nut in a vice. An opposed landing was bound to be fraught with tremendous difficulties and confusion during its first critical hours. How much more difficult would things be if the Luftwaffe had available a hundred or so high-speed fighter-bombers, with which to bomb and strafe the troops coming ashore. A few hours delay in establishing the beachhead might be sufficient for the German Army to move up reserves to defeat the invasion. Hitler's thoughts began to crystallize: what was needed was a ground attack aircraft with the speed to penetrate the powerful fighter defences covering any such invasion. His mind turned towards the only aircraft likely to be available for the task: the Messerschmitt Me 262.

On 2 November Goering, accompanied by Milch and Vorwald, visited the Messerschmitt works at Augsburg to discuss the production of the Me 262. After the *Reichsmarschall* and his entourage had toured the factory complex, Goering mentioned Hitler's requirement for a high-speed fighter bomber and asked whether the Me 262 could carry bombs. Messerschmitt replied: '*Herr Reichsmarschall*, from the very outset we have provided for the fitting of two bomb pylons so it can carry bombs — either one 500 kg or two 250 kgs.'* The head of the company then volunteered the information that the new fighter could even carry two 500 kg or one 1,000 kg (2,200 lb) bomb and went on to state, in answer to a question from Goering, that in his view the task of modifying the fighter to carry bombs could be completed in a couple of weeks.

Just over three weeks later, on 26 November, the Me 262 was demonstrated before Hitler at Insterburg. Inspecting the fourth and sixth prototypes on the ground, the Führer repeated his question: could it carry bombs? Again Messerschmitt assured him in the affirmative: it could carry one 1,000 kg or two 500 kg bombs without difficulty. That was the answer Hitler had sought. Here was the *Blitz-bomber* he was looking for.

From then on the Me 262 featured prominently in Hitler's counter-invasion plans. At a war conference on 20 December he confidently explained to senior Wehrmacht officers:

'Every month that passes makes it more and more probable that we will get at least one *Gruppe* of jet aircraft. The most important thing is that they [the enemy] get some bombs on top of them just as they try to invade. That will force them to take cover, and in this way they will waste hour after hour! But after half a day our reserves will already be on their way. So if we can pin them down on the beaches for just six or eight hours, you can see what that will mean to us ...'

With some modifications the Me 262 could certainly have carried out the role Hitler had in mind for it. There is no evidence that at this stage any Luftwaffe officer tried to sway the Führer from his view. But significantly, Messerschmitt did not initiate work on even a prototype bomb-carrying Me 262. This divergence, between Hitler's expressed wishes and the actual course of development of the Me 262, lit the slow-burning fuse of a time-bomb that was to shake the entire project.

For his part Milch acknowledged the importance of the aircraft as a fighter-bomber but, turning a blind eye to Hitler's wishes, he

---

*A stenographer was present at the conversation and the transcript has survived.

endeavoured to ready the Me 262 for service as a *bomber destroyer* with the minimum of delay. Confirmation of the aircraft in this role came with the maiden flight of the eighth prototype in December 1943, the first to carry armament: it was fitted with a battery of four 30 mm MK 108 cannon, a low velocity weapon whose explosive shells were very effective against bombers but which was not really suitable for ground attack work. Undoubtedly Milch's attitude at this time was influenced by the disturbing intelligence reports he had received on the new generation of US heavy bombers. At a conference in Berlin on 19 January he reviewed the developments to be expected in 1944: 'In this year the new B-29 and B-32 bombers will come into service. They will attack from altitudes of between 11 and 12 km. There is no anti-aircraft gun that can reach such altitudes. The only counter-measure we have is our [future] fighter program. Our present fighters are not able to engage the enemy at such altitudes . . .' In fact the B-29 and the B-32 heavy bombers were never to be used against Germany, and in any case they were incapable of attacking from the '11 and 12 km' altitudes (between about 35,000 and 39,000 feet) predicted by Milch. But the conference minutes provide us with a rare insight into the information (albeit false) on which he was acting. Later in the conference Dr Krome, from Speer's Ministry, asked which was the more important, the V 2 bombardment rocket or the Me 262. Milch snapped back 'We need the Me 262 before all else, before U-boats and tanks, because without this aircraft armament production will no longer be possible . . .'

By the end of January the ninth prototype Me 262 had flown; an additional 23 airframes for the pre-production batch had been completed but lacked engines. Junkers were having considerable difficulty in getting the Jumo 004 into mass production. Not only was the company working very close to the limits of the current technology — the 004 was the first gas turbine in the world to go into large-scale production — but it was having to do so without the steel alloys necessary for high temperature work: chromium and nickel were in desperately short supply in Germany by 1944 and there was insufficient for the mass production of jet engines. Junkers were forced to make an engine that would work using the

substitute materials that were available. For example the combustion chambers of the 004 engine were made out of ordinary steel with a spray coating of aluminium baked on in an oven. As a result failures and fires were a common occurrence with the early production engines, which initially had a running life of only about ten hours. Nearly six months were to pass before the essential solutions to the basic problems had been found and reasonably reliable 004s began to come off the production lines in large numbers. The lack of engines, more than any other factor, imposed a rigid limit to the number of Me 262s completed by the middle of 1944.

As a result of the engine shortages deliveries to the Luftwaffe did not begin until April, when the first 16 were received; during the following month there were only seven. At last sufficient Me 262s were available for the formation of a service trials unit, however, and at the end of April *Erprobungskommando* (Proving Detachment) 262 came into being at Lechfeld in Bavaria, commanded by *Hauptmann* Werner Thierfelder. Thierfelder himself, and several of the other pilots, had come from IIIrd Gruppe of *Zerstoerergeschwader* 26 which flew the bomber-destroyer version of the Messerschmitt Bf 110. *Oberleutnant* Guenther Wegmann, one of the first to join the trials unit, later recalled that he found the Me 262 an easy machine to fly once he had mastered the problem of throttle handling. With the early engines the throttles had to be advanced very slowly indeed, or they were liable to overheat and catch fire. Similarly, once the pilot had cut his throttles at low altitude he was committed to a landing; if he re-opened his throttles and tried to go round again the engines took so long to build up power that the aircraft was likely to hit the ground first. Otherwise Wegmann recalls having little difficulty with flying the Me 262. It must be pointed out, however, that he had had considerable experience with the twin-engined Messerschmitt Bf 110; and he had been trained in instrument flying — a factor whose significance will become clear later. Certainly less-experienced pilots from single-engined day fighter units found the high-speed short-endurance twin-jet Me 262 much more of a handful.

Leutnant 'Quax' Schnoerrer, another of the early pilots, recalled that the usual practice

Starting up and moving away. Above: A ground crewman using the lanyard to start the port Riedel two-stroke starter motor in the nose cone of the Jumo 004 nacelle. The starter could either be started externally in this manner, or electrically from the cockpit. Left: With a high-pitched whine and a burst of flame, the Jumo 004 lights up. Some of the unburnt fuel has fallen on to the hard standing and caught fire. This made it dangerous for jet aircraft to start up on tarmac hardstandings, which were liable to be set on fire. As a result the Luftwaffe was forced to initiate a crash programme to provide the main airfields used by jets with concrete hardstandings. Below: Taxiing out for take-off. This aircraft was one of the early production Me 262s, serial number 170041. *via Bokleman*

was to tow the Me 262 to the take-off point before each flight:

'With fuel for only 40 to 60 minutes flying, one could not spend 10 of them on the ground taxiing. The engines were started up and the throttles advanced very slowly with the wheel brakes on. As soon as the engines reached 8,400 rpm release the brakes, and off we went. Immediately after take-off, at a height of about 10 or 20 metres, bring in the undercarriage and flaps. Once airborne, there was a wonderful feeling of effortless speed and power. But as a result navigation became something of a problem, because by the time one had sorted one's self out after the take-off the aircraft was already several kilometres from the airfild.'

Gradually the pilots of *Erprobungskommando 262* began to amass experience with the new fighter and its temperamental engines, however, and appreciate the enormous advantages in combat of its superb performance: maximum speed 865 kph at 6,000 m (540 mph at about 20,000 feet), initial rate of climb of 20 m/second (3,935 ft per minute). Moreover, the four MK 108 cannon could loose off about 43 kg (96 pounds) of high explosive shells in a three-second burst, giving the Me 262 a fire power considerably higher than any other conventionally-armed German fighter.

It seemed, too, that the Me 262 had become available in the nick of time. By the spring of 1944 the long-range American escort fighters, and in particular the Merlin-engined P-51 which had a performance superior to any German piston-engined equivalent, were escorting bomber formations penetrating deep into Germany. This placed the Luftwaffe fighter force on the horns of an uncomfortable dilemma: if its aircraft carried the heavy armament necessary to knock down the tough B-17s and B-24s, they fell as easy prey if they were caught by the American escorts; but if the German fighters were lightly armed, to enable them to engage the escorts on less unequal terms, they lacked the fire power to knock down the bombers even if they did succeed in penetrating the escorts and getting within range. The Me 262, with both the speed to evade the escorts and the fire-power to tear the bombers to pieces, seemed to provide the only answer to this problem.

In the meantime, however, the slow fuse of the time-bomb under the Me 262 project had burned almost ot its end. On 23 May Goering,

Milch, Galland and other senior Luftwaffe officers, as well as Albert Speer and officials from his armament ministry, were summoned to Berchtesgaden to discuss the latest fighter production programme. For an account of what happened that day the authors are indebted to David Irving*:

"Milch certainly did not suspect the storm was now almost upon him. With *Oberst* Petersen, director of the research establishments, he now joined Goering and Speer in a large unheated room at Hitler's Berghof, with a large picture window overlooking the Alps. Hitler listened absently to the details of the Fighter Staff programme, apparently gazing out over the mountains, until the planning for the Me 262 jet fighter was mentioned. Here he interrupted, 'I thought the 262 was coming as a high-speed bomber? How many of the 262s already manufactured can carry bombs?' Milch told him: 'None *mein Führer*. The Me 262 is being manufactured exclusively as a fighter aircraft.' There was an awkward silence. Milch explained that the aircraft could not carry bombs without extensive design changes, and even then no more than five hundred kilos.

Hitler lost his composure. He now realized that with the Allied invasion in France due any week, the wonder aircraft on which he had rested a large part of his hopes of defeating it could not possibly come in time. He excitedly interrupted Milch, 'Never mind! I wanted only one 250-kilo bomb.' He demanded precise statistics on the loads carried by the fighter version — its armour plate, guns and ammunition. 'Who pays the slightest attention to the orders I give?' he exclaimed. 'I gave an unqualified order, and left nobody in any doubt that the aircraft was to be equipped as a fighter-*bomber*,' "

Not only was Hitler bitterly disappointed at the loss of one of his most important anti-invasion weapons, he was extremely angry at having been deliberately misled about the ability of production Me 262s to carry bombs.

The upshot was that Hitler made Goering personally responsible for getting the Me 262 into service as a fighter-bomber as rapidly as possible, regardless of the effect this would have on the production of the fighter version. During the post-mortem on the day after the Berghof meeting Goering discussed with senior

---

*Published in 'The Rise and Fall of the Luftwaffe: the Life of Luftwaffe Marshal Erhard Milch', Weidenfeld and Nicolson, London.

Top: Me 262 taking off. Because the speed built up rapidly once the aircraft was airborne, it was necessary to retract the undercarriage as soon as possible or a severe nose-down trim change would result. *via Bokleman*

Above and right: Flaps fully down, the Me 262 comes in to land. *via Bokleman*

Left: Me 262 in flight. Because the aircraft was banking at the time the photographs were taken, the dihedral has exaggerated the angle of sweep-back of the wing. *via Bokleman*

Opposite right: Following Hitler's order to prepare the Me 262 for operations as a fighter-bomber, the tenth prototype was used to test the modifications for this role. In this photograph the aircraft carries a single 250 kg (550 lb) bomb on its port rack, and a pair of solid fuel rockets under the rear fuselage to shorten the take-off run. *via Schliephake*

Above: A pair of Me 262 fighter-bombers of *Kommando Schenk* taking off, each carrying two SC 250 bombs under the nose. This unit began operations from Juvincourt in France towards the end of July 1944, and was the first to go into action with turbo-jet propelled aircraft. *via Dierich*

Luftwaffe officers the modifications necessary to ready the Me 262 for the fighter-bomber role. He was told it would mean removing much of the armour plate already in the aircraft, and installing extra fuel tanks under the pilot's seat and in the rear fuselage, as well as installing the bomb pylons. In themselves these were not major modifications, and they could be incorporated in newly-built aircraft relatively easily; but it would be extremely difficult to incorporate these changes to fuselages already built. Goering, who had felt the lash of Hitler's tongue for his failure to ensure the production of the aircraft as a fighter-bomber, now tried to pass on the rebuke: 'The Führer must have the strangest impression of you. From every side, including Messerschmitt, he was left in no doubt about this, right from the start. And then in my presence [at Insterburg] Messerschmitt told the Führer that his company had provided right from the start for it to be manufactured as a fighter-bomber. And now suddenly it is impossible!'

On 27 May Goering telegraphed Milch emphatically: 'The Führer has ordered that the Me 262 aircraft is to enter service exclusively

as a high-speed bomber. The aircraft is not to be regarded as a fighter until further notice.' At a meeting a few days later, however, Hitler relented and agreed to allow testing of the fighter version to continue provided this did not delay the entry into service of the bomb-carrying version. And until further orders only the bomber version was to be delivered to operational units.

The first casualty in the rift over the Me 262 was Erhard Milch himself. Hitler had no further confidence in the man whom he blamed for misleading him, and in the weeks that followed Milch was progressively stripped of his various offices; in retrospect it is remarkable that the Führer did no more than that.

Yet whatever Hitler, Milch, Goering or Messerschmitt had or had not done up till now, the fact remains that the basic factor limiting the production of the Me 262 as a fighter or fighter-bomber was the mass production of the Jumo 004 jet engine. And this had yet to begin. Thus when Allied troops punched their way ashore in Normandy on 6 June, just ten days after the stormy conference at Berchtesgaden, less than thirty Me 262s had been delivered to

the Luftwaffe and neither the aircraft nor its pilots were ready for action. The golden opportunity for the *Blitzbomber* to influence events, if indeed it was capable of doing so, had passed.

In the meantime, work was belatedly begun to convert the Me 262 into a fighter-bomber. The tenth prototype was modified to carry pylons for two 250 kg (550 pound) bombs under the nose. As well as most of the protective armour plating around the pilot, the main fighter-bomber version lost two of its four cannon; strangely, however, the unsuitable 30 mm MK 108 low-velocity cannon was retained as its gun armament. To extend the radius of action, 600 litres (132 Imp gal) of fuel were to be carried in an extra tank fitted in the rear fuselage; but this weighed about as much as the two 250 kg bombs slung under the nose, and the rear tank was well to the rear of the aircraft's centre of gravity. It was imperative, therefore, that this fuel be burnt as early as possible during a combat mission; otherwise, if the bombs were released while the tank was full, the aircraft immediately became dangerously tail-heavy. There were other problems: because of its clean airframe the Me 262 built up speed very rapidly in dive, so it was unsuitable for steep-diving attacks; and because the pilot was unable to see immediately below and ahead of the aircraft to aim his bombs, horizontal attacks from medium or high altitude were likely to be grossly inaccurate. But the Me 262 could be effective at low altitude for horizontal or shallow dive attacks.

For all of its limitations, the Me 262 now fulfilled Hitler's requirement for a high speed counter-invasion fighter-bomber. Its use for this task was to be a temporary expedient, until the more effective Arado Ar 234 bomber became available. This position was confirmed during Hitler's conference on 25 June, after which Albert Speer noted:

'The Führer states again, during a meeting with the *Reichsmarschall* [Goering] his unalterable demand for the immediate production of jet bombers. Until the 234 can be secured in production, series production of the 262 is to be pressed with all speed and it must be made available for this purpose ...'

By this time the first Me 262 fighter-bomber unit, *Erprobungskommando Schenk*, had formed at Lechfeld under the bomber ace *Major* Wolfgang Schenk. Nominally the unit was part of *Kampfgeschwader* 51, from which many of its pilots had come. The hasty conversion on to the new type took almost exactly one month and, on 20 July, the unit moved to Chateaudun near Orleans in France with nine aircraft and pilots in readiness to mount the world's first jet bomber operations.

This continued concentration on the Me

262 as a fighter-bomber, so long after the Allied beachhead in Normandy had been established, might seem to run counter to Hitler's stated aim of using this aircraft against an invasion during its initial stages. But it should be remembered that at this time many German leaders still thought the Normandy landings to be only a feint, to draw German forces away from the Pas de Calais area where the main invasion would take place. And at this time the Allies were mounting a large-scale spoof operation to strengthen the Germans in this impression. If a second invasion operation did take place, *Erprobungskommando Schenk* was to be ready to meet it.

Schenk's fighter-bombers now began spasmodic operations against Allied ground forces but, as a security measure to conserve aircraft to counter the expected main invasion, pilots had strict orders not to attack from altitudes below 4,000 m (about 13,000 feet). Since the Me 262 pilots had no means of aiming their bombs from such an altitude accuracy was poor, and the attacks achieved little. When, in mid-August, the German retreat out of France gathered momentum the detachment, now redesignated Ist *Gruppe* of *Kampfgeschwader*

Airfields used by German jet aircraft in France and Belgium.

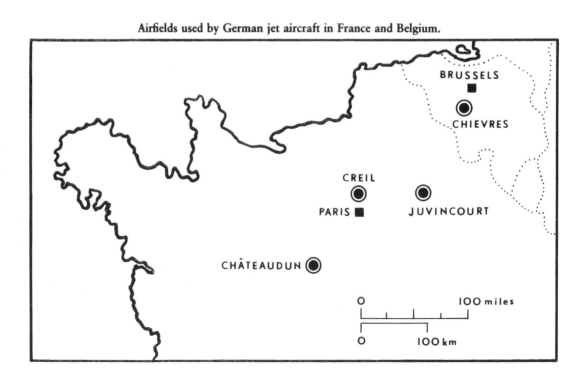

Two stills from an instructional film on the Me 262, showing the aircraft on jacks for a retraction test of the undercarriage. This is a fighter-bomber version, with bomb racks and ports for only two 30 mm cannon. Just in front of the cockpit is the Edelweiss emblem of Kampfgeschwader 51. *via Bokleman*

Above and opposite top: Two more close-ups of an Me 262 fighter-bomber of KG 51, 130179, letter F. *Transit Films*

51, was ordered to pull back to Creil near Paris on 15 August; then to Juvincourt near Rheims on the 22nd, and finally to Chievres in Belgium on 28 August.

It was only on the final day of the withdrawal that Allied fighters made contact with one of the elusive high-speed fighter-bombers. Late on the afternoon of the 28th Major Joseph Myers was leading a flight of P-47s of the 78th Fighter Group, providing top-cover for other aircraft of the Group attacking ground targets. Then, as he later reported:

'While stooging around west of Brussels at 11,000 feet, I caught sight of what appeared to be a B-26, flying at about 500 feet and heading in a southerly direction and going very fast. I immediately started down to investigate and although diving at 45 degrees at 450 IAS [720 kph, indicated airspeed], I was no more than holding my own in regard to the unidentified aircraft. When approximately 5,000 feet above and very nearly directly over the aircraft, I could see that it was not a B-26, although it had

the general overall plan of the B-26. It was painted slate blue in color, with a long rounded nose, but I did not see any guns this time, because at this point he started evasive action, which consisted of small changes of direction not exceeding 90 degrees of turn. The radius of turn was very great and, although I was diving at around 450 IAS, I had very little difficulty cutting him off and causing him to again change direction. He made no effort to climb or turn more than 90 degrees at any time. I closed to within 2,000 feet above him and directly astern and had full power on in a 45 degree dive in an effort to close. At this distance I could readily see the similarity between the aircraft and the recognition plates of the Me 262. With full power on and the advantage of altitude I gradually started closing on the enemy aircraft and drew up to within 500 yards astern and was about to open fire when the enemy aircraft cut his throttle and crash landed in a ploughed field. He hit the ground just as I fired, so I continued firing until within 100 yards of him, observing many strikes around the cockpit and jet units. It skipped over several fields and came to rest and caught fire. The pilot hopped out and started to run.'

Major Joseph Myers, right, forced down an Me 262 of KG 51 near Chievres in Belgium on 28 August 1944, the first Allied pilot to claim one of these aircraft. *USAF*

The German pilot, *Oberfeldwebel* 'Ronny' Lauer of I./KG 51, was able to scramble to safety.

So ended the first phase of the Me 262 fighter-bomber operations. The exaggerated efforts by the Luftwaffe to keep secret the new aircraft had been successful beyond any possible expectation: there is not a single mention in Allied wartime combat reports or intelligence documents of Me 262 fighter-bombers taking any part in the Battle of France. No doubt the ineffectiveness of their bombing attacks contributed to this comforting ignorance.

Meanwhile, deep in Bavaria, *Erprobungskommando 262* had begun operational trials using the Me 262 as a fighter; the targets were the lone Allied reconnaissance aircraft venturing close to the unit's base at Lechfeld. It was during one of the early missions that the commander, *Hauptmann* Werner Thierfelder, lost his life on 18 July under circumstances that are far from clear. German records state that his aircraft was 'shot down' in combat and crashed near Landsberg with the pilot still on board.

But a careful search through British and American records reveals no engagement that links with this loss (and Allied long range reconnaissance aircraft were, in any case, unarmed). A possible cause of the crash is that Thierfelder lost control of his aircraft when he tried to follow a reconnaissance aircraft diving away to escape him.

At full throttle in a shallow dive of about 20 degrees from 8,000 m (26,000 feet), an Me 262 could be well beyond its compressibility threshold of Mach .83 before it had descended through about 2,000 m (7,000 feet). Any increase in speed thereafter resulted in a greatly increased nose-down trim change, requiring considerable backwards pressure on the control column to prevent the dive from steepening uncontrollably; cutting the throttles had no appreciable effect, for the clean-lined jet fighter continued to gather speed in the dive. 'Quax' Schnoerrer recalled an incident during which he had tried to follow down a reconnaissance aircraft and got into such trouble: 'I pulled

A line-up of early production Me 262s of *Erprobungskommando 262* at Lechfeld, probably photographed in July 1944. This unit carried out the trials of this aircraft in the fighter role.

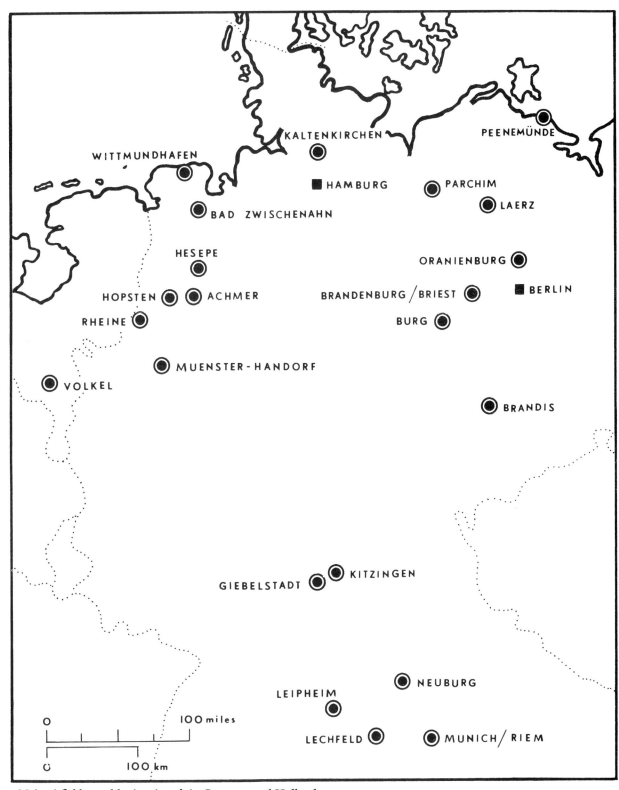

Main airfields used by jet aircraft in Germany and Holland.

Leutnant 'Quax' Schnoerrer joined EKdo 262 soon after its formation, and was credited with 11 kills flying the Me 262 before he himself was shot down and severely wounded on 21 March 1945. *Schoerrer*

back on the stick with all my strength, but the 262 refused to come out of its dive. It was extremely frightening. Finally, in desperation, I jettisoned my canopy; this caused a change of trim, and the aircraft came out of the dive by itself. I landed without my canopy and with the skinning of the wings rippled; the 262 was a write-off.' During the Me 262's combat career, several German pilots had similarly narrow escapes. Others, less fortunate, dived into the ground seemingly for no reason. The slender available evidence suggests that Werner Thierfelder, the world's first jet fighter unit leader, might have fallen to this cause.

There was little time to mourn the fallen commander. Soon after Thierfelder's death his successor arrived at Lechfeld: *Major* Walter Nowotny, an extremely popular young fighter pilot credited with 255 victories on the Eastern Front. The task of gaining operational experience with the new fighter continued.

The first report of an interception by an Me 262 followed one week after Thierfelder's death, on 25 July. Flight Lieutenant A. Wall, RAF, flying a reconnaissance Mosquito of No 544 Squadron, had just carried out a photographic run over Munich at about 9,000 m (30,000 feet) when the jet fighter was first sighted some 400 yards astern. Wall opened his throttles wide and pushed down the nose of the Mosquito to build up his speed, curving steeply to port as he did so. During the next 15 minutes the Me 262 carried out three firing runs on the reconnaissance aircraft. Wall found that even when he used maximum boost the jet fighter easily overhauled him. But he found little difficulty in out-turning his assailant; at

one stage, after three complete turns, Wall found himself on the tail of the Me 262 and could have attacked had his aircraft been armed. Towards the end of the action the Mosquito crew heard two dull thuds and the navigator attempted to open the emergency exit in preparation for baling out, should this prove necessary. With great difficulty he opened the inner hatch, to find that the outer door had disappeared, having broken off near the hinges. In the meantime, however, Wall was able to escape into cloud. The Mosquito landed at Fermo near Ancona in Italy, where the crew found that it had suffered no cannon strikes; but the tip of the port tailplane was

Left: The Rheinmetall Borsig MK 108 carried by the Me 262, with one of its 30 mm rounds. This weapon fired 330 gr (11 oz) high explosive or incendiary rounds at a rate of 660 per minute. This cannon was extremely effective against light metal structures such as aircraft, as shown by the photo above of the effect of a single hit on a Spitfire during a ground firing trial. The low muzzle velocity of only 540 m (1750 ft) per second rendered the weapon unsuitable for strafing ground targets, however.

During July there had been heavy air attacks on the factories producing components for the Me 262, against Leipheim on the 19th and against Regensburg on the 21st. As a result of the shortages of airframe components, and the long-running shortage of engines, the number of Me 262s delivered to the Luftwaffe slumped from 59 in July to only 20 in August.

From a document produced by the Messerschmitt Company, we know that by 10 August 1944 a total of ten prototype Me 262s and 112 production aircraft had been built. Of the former, the 1st, 2nd, 4th, 5th, 6th and 7th prototypes had either been written off or otherwise discarded from the test programme. Twenty-one Me 262s had been destroyed during Allied air raids on the factories; eleven others had been wrecked in accidents or in action. The remaining 84 aircraft were now disposed as follows:

I. *Gruppe* of *Kampfgeschwader* 51 (fighter-bombers)	33
Erprobungskommando 262 (fighters)	15
Rechlin Test Centre	14
Retained at Messerschmitt for flight trials	11
Retained at Junkers for engine trials	1
At Blohm und Voss for conversion to two-seaters	10

With the stabilisation of the battle front in the west early in September, Ist *Gruppe* of *Kampfgeschwader* 51 was able to mount pin-prick attacks against Allied positions from its bases at Rheine and Hopsten just inside Germany. Typical of these was the attack on the forward airfield at Grave, home of No 421 (RCAF) Squadron with Spitfires, on 2 October:

'The attack on the airfield began at 11.00 hours with the dropping of anti-personnel bombs by a jet-propelled aircraft flying at 3,000 ft. In this raid three pilots were injured and one officer and six airmen suffered wounds of minor degree. Several tents were holed and the kit of several officers and airmen badly riddled. Slit trenches were dug and tin hats became fashionable. At noon the second attack came and it was wide of the mark. The third attack resulted in a number of deaths among personnel of the RAF Wing on the other side of the airfield and some Dutch civilians living in the vicinity suffered serious injuries.*

damaged, having almost certainly been struck by the outer door as it broke away. This accounted for the two dull thuds the men had heard. Although the Mosquito had escaped the action was a clear warning to the high-flying Allied reconnaissance crews, that their long run of near-invulnerability over Germany was coming to an end.

During the following month, August, Nowotny's pilots claimed five kills: a Mosquito by *Leutnant* Weber on the 8th, a lone B-17 by *Feldwebel* Lennartz on the 16th, a Lightning by *Oberfeldwebel* Baudach on the 24th, and on the 26th a Spitfire to *Leutnant* Schreiber and a Mosquito to *Oberfeldwebel* Recker.

*Official History: 'The RCAF Overseas, The Sixth Year'

Three days later other Canadian pilots, flying Spitfire IXs of No 401 Squadron, had their revenge. The action was typical of the sort of free-for-all chase that would become common when German jet aircraft were engaged during the months that followed. Sqn Ldr Roy Smith, leading the patrol, afterwards reported:

'I was leading 401 Squadron at 13,000 ft in the Nijmegen area about 5 miles NE of the bridge. We were flying on a NE course when I sighted an Me 262 coming head on 500 ft below. He went into a port climbing turn and I turned starboard after him with several other Spitfires chasing him. He then dived down towards the bridge twisting and turning and half rolling at very high speeds. He flew across Nijmegen turning from side to side. I saw a Spitfire get some strikes on him and he streamed white smoke from the starboard wing root. He flew on at very high speed still and I managed to get behind him and fire two 3 second bursts at 200 to 300 yds approx. He zoomed very high and I saw strikes on him in the port and starboard nacelles ...'

Flight Lieutenant Hedley Everard was one of the others attacking at the same time:

'... I half rolled after it and it started a slow spiral going straight down. I first opened fire from 900 yds and followed it chasing it all the time. At 5,000 ft he began to level out heading south. Throttling back, not to overshoot, I opened fire with machine guns only from 150 yds. A streamer of white smoke came from it and it accelerated rapidly drawing away ...'

Flying Officer John MacKay followed Everard in:

'... I got on the tail of the Me 262 following it down to the ground, firing whenever I could get my sight on the aircraft. Saw strikes on the after part of the fuselage and the port or starboard wing root. The aircraft was extremely manoeuvrable. The pilot was hot and put the aircraft through everything in the book ...'

Flying Officer Gus Sinclair was able to score hits also, before he was crowded out by two other Spitfires diving from above. Then Flight Lieutenant Tex Davenport administered the coup de grâce:

'... I finally closed in to 300 yds astern and emptied the remainder of my guns approx. 10 or 12 seconds into the kite, observing strikes all in engines and fuselage. The aircraft was burning all this time. The pilot seemed to be unhurt and put up a good fight all during this, at the last realising the fight was up he attempted to ram Red 1 [Smith] on the way to the ground where he crashed and burned ...'

The German pilot, *Hauptmann* Hans-Christopf Buttmann of I./KG 51, had indeed aquitted himself well before he was killed in the crash; and in doing so he demonstrated the measure of air superiority necessary to contain the Me 262 menace.

Although the Allied piston-engined fighters could not compete with the Me 262 in terms of maximum horizontal speed and climb, there were often so many about that some were able to attack from above, converting a height advantage into a speed which matched that of the jets. A further advantage enjoyed by the Allied fighter pilots was the newly introduced gyroscopic gunsight, which automatically calculated how far ahead the fighter pilot needed to aim his rounds on a turning or crossing opponent. Designated the Gyro Gunsight Mark II in the Royal Air Force, and the K-14 in the USAAF, the new sight enabled pilots to score hits on high speed crossing targets and greatly increased the overall effectiveness of air-to-air gunnery. The gunsight was used by most of the Canadian pilots during the action on 5 October, and would make a major contribution in many of the successful combats against German jet aircraft during the remainder of the war.

A report circulated round Allied anti-aircraft units in October stated that, of the meagre enemy air activity observed over forward positions in Holland, most was put up by Me 262 fighter-bombers:

'When employed for bombing the aircraft normally makes its run-up in a glide and has, so far during the day, bombed quite indiscriminately mostly with anti-personnel bombs, which though causing some casualties have done little material damage. Normal speed appears to be between 300 and 350 mph and maximum speed of about 500 mph has not normally been used until bombs have been dropped. It has not so far been reported that the aircraft has used its cannon against [ground] targets and if, as is at present believed, the armament is four 30 mm low velocity air-to-air cannon, it is unlikely that it will do so ...'

On 13 October there was a lucky escape for one of the pilots of 1./KG 51. *Unteroffizier* Edmund Delatowski had an inconclusive brush near Volkel with a Royal Air Force Tempest flown by Pilot Officer Robert Cole of No 3 Squadron. Cole ran into the Messerschmitt's slipstream and had to break away, then turned after the jet far in front of him. With the throttle wide open and his aircraft descending in a shallow dive Cole reached 770 kph (480 mph), but even at this speed the Me 262 was pulling away from him slightly. The chase continued eastwards over Holland for about 65 km (40 miles) then, feeling he had shaken off the pursuit, Delatowski slowed his Messerschmitt a little. This was the chance Cole had been waiting for and he closed in to firing range and loosed off a couple of short bursts with his cannon:

'The Messerschmitt appeared to explode like a flying bomb and threw off a number of pieces, including the pilot in a parachute. It went down in a shallow spin and exploded on the ground where the remains burnt out.'

Delatowski parachuted to earth near Deventer, with only minor injuries to the head and left arm.

With the end of the Battle of France, and with it the rescinding of Hitler's insistence that the Me 262 should be used operationally only as a fighter-bomber, the way was at last open for the type to go into action with a front-line fighter unit. By September the problems of mass-producing the Jumo 004 turbo-jet had at last been solved, with the result that during the month a total of 91 Me 262s were delivered to the Luftwaffe.

Kommando Nowotny (as *Erprobungskommando 262* had been re-designated) began to expand to *Gruppe* strength, and by 30 September it possessed 23 Me 262s. Four days later the unit began moving to forward airfields at Achmer and Hesepe, near Osnabrueck in western Germany. The primary target for the jet fighters was to be the American escort fighters covering the bomber attacks; if the former could be forced to jettison their underwing tanks, they could be prevented from covering the bombers on their deep penetration attacks. The bombers could then be engaged more effectively by the German piston-engined fighters. From the start, however, Nowotny had serious problems. Not only did the new fighters still have teething troubles, particularly with the still unreliable jet engines, but the Allies soon learnt the location of the bases operating the jets and began mounting standing patrols over them. Concealment of the airfields being used by the jet aircraft was

impossible: the standard Luftwaffe airfields had asphalt runways, and the asphalt was liable to catch fire when jet aircraft operated off them. So the bases for the jets had to have concrete runways, and this made them readily evident on the photographs brought back by the omniscient Allied reconnaissance aircraft. Once their bases were known it did not take long to establish the 'Achilles heel' of the jet fighters: their vulnerability to attack from conventional fighters when they were flying slowly immediately after take-off or during their approach for landing.

On 7 October *Kommando Nowotny* put up several Me 262s for the first time, to contest a multi-pronged American assault against Poelitz, Ruhland, Magdeburg, Kassel and Zwickau. First Lieutenant Urban Drew, flying a P-51 of the 361st Fighter Group, was escorting one of the B-17 formations passing almost over Achmer when he spotted two Me 262s taxiing out to take off:

'The lead ship was in take-off position on the east-west runway and the taxiing ship got into position for a formation take-off. I waited until they both were airborne and then I rolled over from 15,000 ft and headed for the attack with my Flight behind me. I caught up with the second Me 262 when he was about 1,000 ft off the ground; I was indicating 450 mph and the jet aircraft could not have been going over 200 mph. I started firing from about 400 yds, 30 degrees deflection. As I closed on him, I observed hits all over the wings and fuselage. Just as I passed him I saw a sheet of flame come out near the right wing root. As I glanced back I saw a gigantic explosion and a sheet of red-orange flame shot out over an area of about 1,000 ft. The other jet aircraft was about 500 yds ahead of me and had started a fast climbing turn to the left. I was still indicating about 400 mph and I had to haul back on the stick to stay with him. I started shooting from about 60 degrees deflection, 300 yds, and my bullets were just hitting the tail section of the enemy aircraft. I kept horsing back on the stick and my bullets crept up the fuselage to the cockpit. Just then I saw the canopy go flying off in two sections and the plane rolled over and went into a flat spin. He hit the ground on his back at about a 60 degree angle.'

One of the German pilots, *Leutnant* Gerhard Kobert, was killed in the action. The other, *Oberleutnant* Paul Bley, managed to bale out and escaped without injury.

In the meantime other Me 262s of *Kom-*

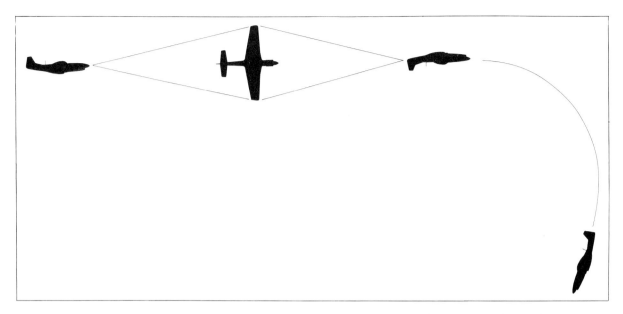

The 'Split-S' manoeuvre, employed by fighters wishing to pick up speed rapidly to engage an enemy below. It was frequently used by P-51 pilots trying to catch German jet aircraft.

Opposite top, and below: Messerschmitt 262s of *Kommando Nowotny*, photographed in the autumn of 1944. Almost certainly these pictures were taken at Lechfeld in Bavaria where the unit was working up for operations; to have lined up aircraft like this at any of the airfields in western Germany at this time would have invited their immediate destruction by Allied fighter-bombers. The half-track *Kettenkrad* vehicle was widely used by the Luftwaffe for towing aircraft. *via Bokleman*

mando Nowotny were climbing to engage the bomber formations and Nowotny himself, *Oberfaehnrich* Heinz Russel and *Feldwebel* Heinz Lennartz each claimed a B-24. After his victory, however, Russel was engaged by a pair of P-47s of the 479th Fighter Group flown by Colonel Hubert Zemke and Lieutenant Norman Benolt and shot down; the German pilot baled out and landed without injury.

Thus, during its first real action, *Kommando Nowotny* had lost three Me 262s shot down and one pilot killed, for a claim of three American bombers. It was hardly an impressive ratio, but it was one that would become common as the German jet fighters were sent into action against a foe greatly superior numerically.

Between the beginning of October and the end of the first week in November 1944 *Kommando Nowotny* claimed to have shot down four American heavy bombers (all B-24s), twelve fighters (P-47s and P-51s) and three reconnaissance aircraft. During the same period the unit lost six Me 262s in combat and seven destroyed; nine others were damaged in accidents.

On 4 October *Oberleutnant* Alfred Teumer was killed attempting to land his Me 262 with one engine flamed out; and on the 28th *Oberleutnant* Paul Bley suffered fatal injuries when, shortly after take-off, he ran into a flock of birds and both engines flamed out. Two other Me 262s were wrecked during attempted single-engine landings; three were wrecked and one damaged in other take-off and landing accidents; one was wrecked and four damaged following emergency landings after running short of fuel; two were damaged following a partial or total failure of the undercarriage to extend; and one suffered damage but no records appear to exist of the cause. On 29 October *Leutnant* Alfred Schreiber collided with the Spitfire reconnaissance aircraft he was intercepting; both aircraft were destroyed, but Schreiber was able to bale out.

Oberfeldwebel Willi Banzaff was lucky to escape with his life during the action on 1 November. As American heavy bombers were withdrawing after attacking Gelsenkirchen and Ruedesheim, he carried out a lone attack on P-51s of the 20th Fighter Group and shot down one of them. Banzaff continued towards the B-17s bent on engaging them also. But by that time the P-51s of 20th FG were diving after him in vengeful pursuit, as were others of the 352nd FG and P-47s of the 56th FG. Suddenly the sky seemed alive with American fighters scrambling to get into a firing position on the lone jet fighter. Banzaff descended rapidly to 3,000 m (10,000 ft) then turned away at high speed towards the north, trying to outrun his pursuers. In turning, however, he gave some of the diving American fighters the chance to cut him off. The P-47s and P-51s opened fire at long range and hits were scored on the fuselage and left wing. Lieutenant Walter Groce of the 56th FG called over the radio 'Spread out and we'll get him if he turns!' Shortly afterwards Banzaff did turn, giving Groce the chance he had been waiting for. He made the most of it. Then, in the terse wording of the 56th FG report: 'After repeated hits jet started to smoke; pilot jettisoned canopy and baled out, 8,000 ft. Two unidentified P-51s in vicinity shot at pilot on chute.' Credit for shooting down the Me 262 was shared between Groce and Lieutenant William Gerbe of the 352nd FG. In spite of the unchivalrous conduct of two of his foes, Banzaff reached the ground safely.

Three days later, on 4 November, Banzaff was in action again but this time his luck ran out. German records state that he was shot down and killed in action with enemy fighters, but a careful check through Allied records reveals no claim that links with this.

The initial complement of pilots of *Erprobungskommando 262* had comprised experienced pilots, many of them from twin-engined fighter units, who had had a full training in instrument flying. In *Kommando Nowotny*, however, some of the pilots had come from single-engined fighter units and lacked proper training in instrument flying (the normal training programme for German single-engined fighter pilots included only a rudimentary training in this). For these men the Me 262, with its high speed, short endurance and compressibility problems if too rapid a descent was made, was not an easy machine to handle. Add to this the almost continual harassment from Allied fighters patrolling near the bases, and the fine judgement necessary for landing the aircraft because of the poor throttle response of the engines, and one can see that there were

several traps awaiting the less-experienced pilot. The result was that, in spite of the high hopes entertained for the Me 262 as a fighter, its first month of operations in this role had been disappointing. Tangible success remained tantalisingly beyond the grasp of Nowotny's *Kommando*.

Then, on 8 November, disaster struck the jet fighter unit. It had sent up several Me 262s to engage a large force of American bombers returning after an attack on the Mitteland Canal, and these scored some kills: *Leutnant* Franz Schall claimed the destruction of three P-51s and *Oberleutnant* Guenther Wegmann claimed one more. But shortly after Schall's last kill Lieutenant James Kenney of the 357th Fighter Group was able to get into a firing position and he hit the Messerschmitt with an accurate burst which jammed both throttles. Schall was forced to bale out. Shortly afterwards, Nowotny himself was in trouble. Lieutenant Edward Haydon, also of the 357th was returning from a strafing attack near Hanover when he caught sight of an Me 262 descending south of Dummer Lake:

'I gave chase drawing maximum power, and as I was beginning to close on the 262 I was slowly over-taken by ships of the 20th Fighter Group. At this time the 262 led us across an airfield south of Dummer Lake which immediately let go with all of its flak at us. The Me 262 pulled up and rolled over on its back, crashing about 100 feet in front of me, at which time I was about 50 feet high. The pilot was not seen to bale out.'

The 'airfield south of Dummer Lake' was almost certainly Achmer. The leading P-51 of the 20th FG was that flown by Captain Ernest Fiebelkorn. Nowotny's final radio call stated

Opposite, top: First Lieutenant Urban Drew who, flying a P-51 of the US 361st Fighter Group, destroyed two Me 262s of *Kommando Nowotny* on 7 October shortly after they had taken off from Achmer. *USAF via Hess*

Opposite, centre: Captain Ernest Fiebelkorn of the 20th Fighter Group, one of the American pilots who was chasing Nowotny when the latter's Me 262 suddenly dived into the ground. *Fiebelkorn via Hess*

Right: *Major* Walter Nowotny, the commander of the first Me 262 fighter unit to be declared fully operational, was killed in action on 8 November under circumstances that are far from clear. Probably he was shot down in error by the flak defences at Achmer. *Schnoerrer*

'*Ich bin getroffen*' — 'I've been hit', but it is not clear whether this meant the aircraft, or Nowotny himself, had been hit. Shortly afterwards Nowotny's Me 262 dived into the ground about four miles north of Achmer; the position links with that mentioned in Haydon's report. During the action *Kommando Nowotny* lost two Me 262s—Schall's and Nowotny's—and no other Me 262 unit reported losing a pilot during the day. There is clear evidence, therefore, that the Me 262 pursued by Haydon and Fiebelkorn had been Nowotny's. But the question remains: who fired the fatal burst? Neither of the American pilots had managed to get into position to open fire on the jet fighter, and no other Allied pilot reported a combat that can be linked with it. The meagre evidence available suggests that the German fighter ace was shot down in error by the Achmer flak defences.

Generalmajor Adolf Galland had actually been at Achmer on 8 November, visiting Nowotny to assess the effectiveness of his *Kommando*. The General saw enough to realise that Nowotny had been given an almost impossible task: to bring into service a completely new fighter with several novel features, using pilots in many cases without a proper conversion training, and all of that from airfields close to the front line in an area in which the enemy enjoyed massive numerical superiority. Adolf Galland's reaction was characteristically decisive: he ordered the unit to return to Lechfeld in Bavaria, to re-form and undergo further training.

Kommando Nowotny's new commander was *Major* Erich Hohagen and, on 24 November, it was re-designated IIIrd *Gruppe* of *Jagdgeschwader* 7. Initially the new *Geschwader* took the honorary title 'Hindenburg', from the recently disbanded bomber unit *Kampfgeschwader* 1; but soon afterwards it was renamed *Jagdgeschwader Nowotny* after its fallen leader.

Once back in the relative safety of Bavaria, III./JG 7 was able to devote itself to the essential task of improving the level of training of the less experienced pilots. And there were the regular overflights by Allied reconnaissance aircraft, on which the German pilots could practice their skills. Typical of these actions was that on 26 November, when *Major* Rudolf Sinner took off to intercept a reconnaissance

P-38 escorted by three P-38 fighters engaged in a high altitude photographic mission over Munich. The reconnaissance pilot, Lieutenant Renne, had just completed his run over the target when he spotted Sinner's Me 262 closing on him rapidly. Renne immediately called in his escorting fighters, released his drop tanks, opened his throttles wide and turned into his assailant to give the most difficult deflection shot. The two aircraft passed each other almost head-on without Sinner being able to open fire, then Renne wheeled his Lightning round in a tight turn to the right in an endeavour to meet the next attack head-on also. By now, however, the escorting P-38s were closing in on Sinner who was forced to break away sharply. In doing so the German pilot pushed down the nose of his Me 262 too steeply and then, to his horror, found himself going down out of control: in his haste to escape he had gone over the aircraft's compressibility threshold. After several hair-raising seconds wrestling with his control column, Sinner finally succeeded in extricating the Me 262 from its dive by the use of his tailplane trim control. The German pilot glanced back at his foes and caught sight of them high above and far to the north of him, leaving long condensation trails as they regained formation and headed southwards for their bases in Italy. Bravely, in view of his own recent narrow escape, Sinner resolved to go after them. He pushed open his throttles and this time the rapidly climbing jet fighter was able to move unseen into a firing position behind one of the escorting P-38s. 'The burst from my four 3 cm cannon scored hits on the tail and the right wing. It rolled over on its back and went down burning, in a turn to the left,' Sinner later recalled. 'I pulled up and turned left for home, heading for Lechfeld now short of fuel.' The American pilot, Lieutenant Julius Thomas, baled out and landed near Kitzbuehl where he was taken prisoner.

Following the difficulties experienced by *Kommando Nowotny*, as a result of the over-hasty conversion of pilots on to the Me 262, towards the end of November a formalised training programme was introduced. IIIrd *Gruppe* of *Ergaenzungs Jagdgeschwader* 2 was re-formed at Lechfeld as an operational conversion unit for new Me 262 pilots under the fighter ace *Oberstleutnant* Heinz Baer. The conversion began with 20 hours flying on conventional fighters with their throttles fixed, to accustom the pilots to the problem of flying an aircraft whose throttles could not be adjusted in flight at high altitude (if this was attempted in the Me 262 the engines were liable to flame-out). All the pilots then received three days' theoretical instruction in the operation and handling of the jet engines. Next, those pilots without experience of twin-engined aircraft were sent on a short course at Landsberg; there they received five hours flying in the Messerschmitt Bf 110 and the Siebel Si 204, concentrating on the problems of asymmetric flight. There was a further day's theoretical instruction on the Me 262, after which the embryo jet pilots received some ten hours flying and gunnery training on the Me 262. The men were then pronounced fit for combat, and were sent to the operational units. It was only a cursory training, especially as some of the pilots came straight from advanced pilot training having never flown on an operational unit. But it was certainly better than what had gone before and, given the desperate position in which Germany now found herself, the best that was possible.

One further problem that now exercised the Luftwaffe High Command was that of providing for the Me 262 fighter units pilots with an adequate training in instrument flying. The American heavy bombers, equipped with radar, were able to navigate to and attack targets even though the route from their bases was blanketed by cloud. This meant that on many occasions the German fighters would have to be able to climb and descend through cloud, if they were to provide an effective defence. As we have observed, the normal training for German single-engined fighter pilots had not included a full instruction in instrument flying (though some pilots later received it). Yet a rapid descent through cloud in the Me 262 was an operation fraught with difficulties for pilots without such training, with the fearful phenomenon of compressibility always waiting to snatch at the unwary. Obviously, given sufficient time, the newer pilots could have received the necessary additional training in instrument flying. But time was short and so was fuel.

By the end of 1944 there was, however, a large pool of instrument-trained pilots available to the Luftwaffe: those who had belonged to the bomber units, most of which had had to be disbanded in the previous summer due to the shortage of fuel. The idea now arose that many of these men could be used to fly the Me 262 in action, *as a fighter*. It was felt that the ex-bomber pilots, with considerable experience of both instrument flying and multi-engined aircraft, would be better able to handle the Me 262 on cloudy days than those from the German single-engined fighter units lacking instrument training. That the ex-bomber pilots had not been trained or given experience in aerial combat in the fighter role was accepted as a drawback but not an overriding one: these Me 262s were intended not to dog-fight with the enemy fighters, but to go straight in and knock down the enemy four-engined bombers. The idea of using the ex-bomber pilots in this way was supported by *Oberst* Gordon Gollob, *Oberst* Dietrich Peltz and, more importantly, by General Karl Koller who was the Chief of the Luftwaffe General Staff and also by Goering. It was bitterly opposed by *Generalmajor* Adolf Galland and several of the fighter leaders, who felt that turning over the Me 262s to pilots untrained in fighter operations was a major blunder. Several later accounts have linked this controversy with Hitler's earlier order that the Me 262 should be used only as a fighter-bomber; the two issues were, however, entirely separate. The authors have examined the evidence regarding the operation of the Me 262 by ex-bomber pilots carefully and believe that there are cogent arguments on both sides.

In the death throes of the Third Reich, with enemy forces now massing in the east, the west and the south for the final push into Germany itself, the question of which pilots were to operate the Me 262 sparked off a major clash within the operational High Command of the Luftwaffe. The upshot was that, as a result of this and other disagreements with Goering,

Generalmajor Galland was dismissed his post as Inspector of Fighters. And the re-equipping of some of the ex-bomber units with the Me 262 went ahead: the first such unit, *Kampfgeschwader (Jaeger) 54*, began its conversion at Giebelstadt at the end of November. Three further ex-bomber units, *Kampfgeschwader 6, 27 and 55*, were scheduled to receive the jet fighter early in 1945.

During the final three months of 1944 a total of 342 Me 262s were built, which meant that sufficient were now available for other roles. In November *Kommando Welter* was formed, a night fighter unit based at Burg near Magdeburg under the command of *Oberleutnant* Kurt Welter. Initially the unit had only two Me 262s, both single seaters, one of which was fitted with the pilot-operated FuG 218 *Neptun* radar. The primary targets for these first jet night fighters were the fast high-flying Mosquito bombers of the Royal Air Force, which until now had been able to attack their targets with little risk of interception. Also at this time *Kommando Brauegg* was formed, a short-range reconnaissance unit under the command of *Hauptmann* Brauegg. For this role the Me 262 was fitted with a re-designed nose section, with the guns removed and two Rb 50/30 aerial cameras mounted to look downwards and outwards. To accommodate the tops of the cameras and their film magazines, two large tear-drop fairings were fitted just ahead of the cockpit of this version; in addition a window was cut in the floor of the cockpit to enable the pilot to sight his cameras on ground features vertically underneath the aircraft.

Layout of cameras in the nose of the reconnaissance version of the Me 262, positioned on either side of the retracted nose wheel.

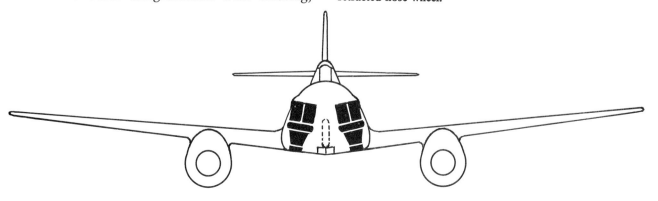

Top: A reconnaissance Me 262, probably belonging to *Kdo Brauegg*, airborne with its undercarriage lowered.

Opposite, top: Me 262 fighter-bomber of KG 51 being towed out at Rheine, late in 1944. *Goetz*

Left: Single-seat Me 262 fitted with Neptun radar and nose-mounted aerials, tested in action by *Oberleutnant* Kurt Welter at the end of 1944. *via Creek*

Below: An Me 262 with collapsed nose gear at Lechefeld. This photo is of particular interest because it is one of the very few to show an aircraft in German markings with the nose bulge for the vertically mounted camera; almost certainly the aircraft belonged to *Kommando Brauegg*.

At the close of 1944, however, the great majority of Me 262 sorties were still being flown by the fighter-bombers of *Kampfges-chwader* 51. The Ist *Gruppe* flew from Rheine and Hopsten while the IInd *Gruppe*, which had recently commenced operations after re-equipping with the Me 262, flew from Hesepe. On 16 December the German army opened its last offensive of the war, in the Ardennes area, and the Me 262s were frequently committed against Allied troop concentrations and supply centres. As a counter to these operations, the Allied fighter forces mounted numerous stand-ing patrols over the battle area. There is little evidence that the fleeting hit-and-run attacks by the jet fighter-bombers caused any signi-ficant damage. Probably their greatest effect was that by pinning down the enemy fighters in this way *Kampfgeschwader* 51 prevented them from bombing and strafing German troops. During the grim closing months of the war, it was the nearest thing to air support the bat-tered German army could expect.

On New Year's Day 1945 the Luftwaffe gambled almost the whole of its fighter force in the west in a massive all-out attack by nearly a thousand aircraft on Allied airfields in France, Holland and Belgium. Taking part in the attack were some twenty Me 262s of KG 51, assigned to the airfields at Eindhoven and Heesch in Holland. The Eindhoven attack, made in con-cert with Messerschmitt Bf 109s and FW 190s of *Jagdgeschwader* 3, proved to be the most successful of the entire operation and caused destruction or damage to more than fifty Spitfires and Typhoons of the three Wings based on the airfield. In contrast the attack on Heesch, made in concert with *Jagdgeschwader* 6, achieved little. At least two Me 262s were lost during the action, one of which fell to ground fire near Heesch.

During the first weeks of 1945 *Kampfges-chwader* 51 mounted attacks against Allied positions whenever the poor weather allowed, in conjunction with the Arado Ar 234s of *Kampfgeschwader* 76. On 10 January there

Top and left: The *Deichselschlepp* (pole-tow) airborne trailer, tested with the tenth prototype Me 262, as a method of increasing the bomb load this aircraft could carry. The wing was taken from a V1 flying bomb. The towing bar was about 6 m (19 ft) long and the swivel fitted to the tail of the Me 262 allowed both horizontal and vertical movement of the trailer in flight. Electrically fired explosive bolts were fitted to enable the pilot to jettison the dolly undercarriage after take-off, release the bomb on the target, and jettison the trailer. During the flight trials carrying a 1,000 kg (2,200 lb) bomb in this manner considerable difficulties were experienced with 'porpoising' of the trailer and the movement being transmitted to the aircraft via the towing bar. During one such trial flight test pilot Gerd Lindner lost control of his Me 262 and had to bale out. During another trial a turn by the towing aircraft imposed excessive loads on the towing swivel, which tore away from the rear fuselage. On yet another trial the explosive bolts failed to function, but Lindner skilfully landed the Me 262 with the trailer and bomb still attached. In the end the trials were abandoned, the method being described as 'hazardous and unsatisfactory'. *via Schliephake*

Left: Two Me 262s were modified as high altitude horizontal bombers, with the guns removed and a specially constructed wooden and perspex nose cone to house a bomb-aimer lying on his stomach and a Lotfe tachometric bombsight. The aircraft carried the same bomb load, two SC 250 bombs, as the normal fighter-bomber version. The trials with the type appear not to have been successful, however, and no further aircraft were modified in this way. *via Heise*

Bottom: The horizontal bomber version being towed by a refuelling vehicle. *via Creek*

were 22 jet bomber sorties against Strasbourg; on the 23rd there were thirty more against the same target.

By the beginning of 1945 a total of 564 Me 262s had been accepted by the Luftwaffe and production was running at about 36 per week. Yet the Luftwaffe Quartermaster General's records for 10 January listed only about 61 of these aircraft in service with operational units, distributed as follows:

I. and II./KG 51 (fighter-bombers)	52
10./NJG 11 (night-fighters)	approx. 4
Kommando Brauegg (short-range recce)	5

Probably three times as many more were distributed amongst the units working up to go into action or training pilots: the three *Gruppen* of *Jagdgeschwader* 7, KG (J) 54, the conversion unit III./Erg. JG 2, and the various test centres. By then an estimated 150 Me 262s had been destroyed in the air or on the ground by enemy action, or in accidents. Taken together, this accounts for some 400 Me 262s and the figures are, if anything, on the high side. By that date, however, the Luftwaffe had accepted some 600 Me 262s from the makers and it is interesting to speculate on the whereabouts of the remaining 200 aircraft, one third of the total. Without doubt a large number of the remainder were tied up in the German rail system: surprisingly, until very late in the war, the majority of Me 262s were dismantled after their acceptance test flights and sent to the operational units *by rail*; from now until the end of the war a large proportion of the Allied bomber attacks were aimed at systematically dismantling the German rail network, with the result that many Me 262s simply got lost in transit.

It is interesting to note that on 10 January the Quartermaster General's list recorded no Me 262 *day fighters* in service with operational units; this was *four months* after Hitler had released the Me 262 for service in this role. At this time III./JG 7 was at full strength but still working up, with one *Staffel* each at Brandenburg-Briest, Oranienburg and Parchim, all in the Berlin area. I./JG 7 under *Major* Desdorffer was forming at Kaltenkirchen near Hamburg, as was II./JG 7 under *Major* Erich Rudorffer at Briest. At the same time, further south, I./KG (J) 54 was hastily converting on to the Me 262 at Giebelstadt near Wuerzburg.

The first of the Me 262 units declared ready for the new phase of jet fighter operations was I./KG (J) 54, which put up about ten machines on 9 February to counter a multi-pronged American attack on targets at Magdeburg, Weimar, Lutzkendorf, Bielefeld, Paderborn, Arnsberg and Dulmen involving more than 1,500 heavy bombers. The result was a utter defeat for the German unit, whose ex-bomber pilots had been sent into action with only the sketchiest training and without ever having had any gunnery practice in the Me 262. P-51 Mustangs of the 78th, 357th and 359th Fighter Groups claimed five Me 262s destroyed during the action, for one B-17 damaged. In fact I./KG (J) 54 lost six Me 262s on that day, only one of which can be linked with certainty to an American combat report. Lieutenant John Carter of the 357th FG later reported that, as he was on a bomber escort mission in the vicinity of Fulda at about 7,400 m (24,000 feet) his squadron encountered the jet fighters:

'Cement Blue Flight leader dropped his tanks immediately and made an attack on the four Me 262s that were low and to our left. The Me 262s split, two going to the right and two to the left. Cement Blue leader took one of the Me 262s that went to the right and I took the other. I followed the jet that I was after for about ten or fifteen minutes. I got in some good bursts at him but he was out of range and gaining distance on me all the time. I was still after this jet when I spotted another Me 262 about 12,000 to 15,000 feet below me and he appeared to be in a glide. I gave up the one that I was chasing at the time, rolled over and split-essed on the one below me. I gained on him very rapidly and gave him several bursts. I was out of range, but saw a few strikes. I was still closing on him when the pilot baled out.

This claim links with the loss of the Me 262 piloted by *Major* Ottfried Sehrt, the commander of I./KG (J) 54, who parachuted to earth north of Frankfurt with a bullet through his shin; the wound was not serious, however, and less than a week later he was back with his unit. The commander of the *Geschwader*, *Oberstleutnant* Baron Volprecht von Riedesel, was less fortunate: he was still on board his Me 262 when it plunged into the ground near Limburg, following his action with the raiding force.

Just over two weeks later there was another

bad day for KG (J) 54, this time for the newly formed IInd *Gruppe*. On the morning of the 25th, as four of the unit's Me 262s were getting airborne for a training flight, they were spotted by Mustangs of the 55th Fighter Group. Captain Don Penn, leading a fighter sweep through the area, afterwards reported seeing the jets taking off from Giebelstadt:

'We were flying at 13,000 feet, and I ordered the Squadron to drop tanks and engage the enemy aircraft. I dived on one jet, using 50 inches of Mercury and 3,000 rpm. He was making a slight turn to port at 1,000 feet heading back toward the drome, so I levelled off about 3,000 yards behind him and put on full power. My indicated airspeed was then about 500 mph and I expected him to use full power also and attempt to pull away from me. However I closed rapidly, firing from 1,000 yards. At 500 yards I observed the 262 to have its wheels down. I cut down on my power and at 300 yards started striking the enemy aircraft in the right power unit. Closing to 50 yards, I broke sharply over the top of the jet, watching him as he rolled over and went straight in and exploded.'

Other pilots in Penn's squadron also engaged the slow flying jets, shooting down two others. *Leutnants* Hans Knobel and Josef Lackner, and *Feldwebel* Heinz Klausner, were killed during the brief encounter. Altogether KG (J) 54 lost 12 Me 262s on that day, six in air combat, two as a result of technical failures and four on the ground during a strafing attack.

Von Riedesel's replacement as commander of KG (J) 54 was *Major* Hans-Georg Baetcher, a distinguished bomber pilot who had previously flown Arado Ar 234 jet bombers with KG 76. When Baetcher took over the *Geschwader* its three *Gruppen* had between them about twenty Me 262s based at Giebelstadt, Kitzingen and Neuburg. 'KG (J) 54 had been declared ready for operations prematurely,' Baetcher recalled. 'The first thing I did was to order further training. The main problem was to get the ex-bomber pilots used to the much greater speed — the 262 cruised two or three times faster than the Ju 88s or He 111s the pilots had flown previously. Also we had only single-seat Me 262s, no two seaters. On the other hand the pilots on the unit all had quite a lot of flying experience and so were able to cope with problems that might have been too much for a less experienced man.' In spite of the difficulties experienced by the ex-bomber

pilots during their early combats, Baetcher still feels that in the circumstances the decision to employ men with blind flying training to operate the Me 262 was correct, especially during the winter when cloud prevented the other jet fighter units from operating. 'The biggest error,' he felt, 'was that the German fighter pilots had not been trained in blind flying in the first place.'

It was not until the third week in February that III./JG 7 was considered ready for action again; but now, having had time to bring its pilots up to a higher standard of training, the unit was considerably more proficient in combat. On 21 February Mustangs of the 479th Fighter Group were patrolling the Berlin area when they encountered an estimated fifteen Me 262s which behaved quite differently from those previously encountered:

'Bounce was directed at Red Flight, as squadron was making a shallow turn to the left from an easterly direction. Bounce came from 3 o'clock position at our level by four Me 262s flying the usual American combat formation, looking like P-51s with drop tanks. Our Red Flight broke into jets but they crossed in front of our flight up and away. A second flight of four Me 262s flying in American combat formation then made a bounce

Oberstleutnant **Baron Volprecht von Riedesel, the commander of KG (J) 54, who was killed in action with American fighters on 9 February 1945.** *via Rehm*

Below: Variously captioned in the past, this photograph depicts Me 262s of Kampfgeschwader (Jaeger) 54 at Giebelstadt early in 1945. Almost certainly the aircraft on the left had started life as a fighter-bomber version; hence the unusual camouflage scheme and only one gun port on each side of the nose, though the bomb racks have been removed. *Baetcher*

from the rear, 6 o'clock high. Our flight turned into this second Me 262 flight and the Me 262s broke climbing up and away. At this time the first flight of Me 262s came back on us again from above and to the rear. We broke into this flight and this kept up for three or four breaks, neither ourselves or Jerry being able to get set or close in for a shot. Each time we would break they would climb straight ahead outdistancing us. Within the Jerry flight the number 4 man, while turning, would fall behind and slightly above, so that it was necessary to take on this number 4 man or he would slice in on our tail if our Flight would take on the rest of the Jerry flight.'

The American pilots noted that the German pilots '... were aggressive and experienced. They were not caught in a turn, and if they were caught in such a position would roll out and climb up and away. It was impossible to catch or climb with them.' It seemed that the German pilots' aim, during the inconclusive combat, was to force the Mustangs to drop their external fuel tanks so that they would have to leave the area; in this they were unsuccessful, however, for the American pilots were able to ward off the repeated attacks with the tanks still on their wings. The report illustrated well the sort of inconclusive action likely to result when well-handled jets confronted well-handled Mustangs; the Me 262 was no real threat to the latter. But there was no doubt that the jet fighter posed a considerable threat to the American bombers, for with its high speed it could pierce the screens of escorting Mustangs with relative ease.

During February the most successful German jet fighter pilot was *Leutnant* Rudolf Rademacher of III./JG 7. After shooting down a Spitfire reconnaissance aircraft near Brunswick on the 1st, he was credited with a B-17 on the 4th, two more on the 8th and one on the 14th, a P-51 on the 16th, a further B-17 on the 23rd and a B-24 on the 25th, making his score for the month eight kills.

Near the end of February a new and potentially very effective Me 262 fighter unit was formed under the command of *Generalmajor* Adolf Galland, following his recent removal from the post of Inspector of Fighters: *Jagdverband 44*. The official order for its formation, dated 24 February, stated:

'JV 44 is established at Brandenburg-Briest with immediate effect. Ground personnel are to be drawn from 16./JG 54, Factory Protection Unit 1

and III./Erg JG 2. The commander of this unit receives the disciplinary powers of a Divisional Commander as laid down in Luftwaffe Order 3/9.17. It is subordinated to Luftflotte Reich and comes under *Luftgaukommando* III (Berlin). Operational *Verband* 'Galland' is to have a provisional strength of 16 operational Me 262s and 15 pilots.
   signed *Generalleutnant* Karl Koller
   Chief of the General Staff of the Luftwaffe.'

  Behind this terse order was the establishment of one of the most remarkable fighter units ever formed. That it should have been commanded by a general was only one of its unique features; for now, with the German conventional fighter units able to operate only rarely due to the shortage of fuel, Galland was able to draw to JV 44 several of the most experienced and successful fighter pilots in the Luftwaffe. As he later commented, 'The *Ritterkreuz* was, so to speak, the badge of our unit.' In addition to Galland himself with this covetted decoration, there were *Oberst* Johannes Steinhoff, *Oberst* Guenther Luetzow, *Oberstleutnant* Heinz Baer, *Majors* Gerhard Barkhorn, Erich Hohagen, Karl-Heinz Schnell and Willi Herget, *Hauptmann* Walter Krupinski, *Oberleutnant* Hans Gruenberg, and *Leutnants* Klaus Neumann and Heinz Sachsenberg. But even a unit with this level of expertise took time to set up in the final chaos of the Third Reich, and not until the end of March would it be ready

Top, and opposite: R4M 55 mm high explosive rockets, mounted in twelves on wooden racks under the wings of the Me 262. The rockets had approximately the same trajectory as the rounds from the MK 108 cannon, so both weapons could be aimed using the normal Revi sight without adjustment. The tail of the R4M had eight fins which extended after launch. *via Schliephake*

Above: Personnel of Jagdgeschwader 7: *Oberleutnant* Guenther Wegmann (wearing white jacket) and *Leutnant* Joachim Weber, two successful pilots with the unit credited with eight and six kills respectively flying the Me 262; Wegmann was seriously injured in action on 18 March 1945, Weber was killed in action three days later. The other two men in the photograph, *Oberleutnant* Fred Leitner (left) and *Feldwebel* Hans Zeller (far right) were fighter controllers attached to JG 7. *Wegmann*

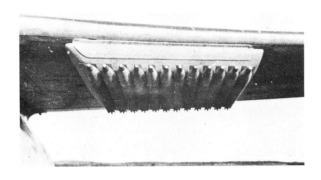

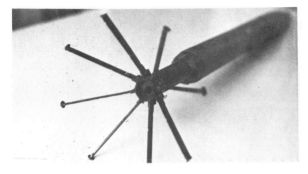

for action.

Meanwhile, during February, *Kampfges-chwader* 51 continued to put up more operational sorties with its fighter-bombers than all the other Me 262 units put together. One of the strongest reactions was on 14 February, when more than 55 jet bombers took part in attacks against British forces advancing near Kleve. Three of the Me 262s were caught and shot down by prowling fighters of the 2nd Tactical Air Force, two of them on the way to their target by Typhoons of No 439 Squadron RCAF; when it still had its bombs on board, the Me 262 was slowed sufficiently for it to be caught by conventional fighters. Flight Lieutenant L. Shaver later reported:

'I was leading a section of four aircraft of 439 Squadron on an armed recce of the Coesfeld-Enschede area. While flying west at 7,000 feet at approximately 20 miles from Coesfeld, I observed two Me 262s line abreast flying west at 3,000 feet. I informed the other pilots and dived to attack. I came in line astern slightly below the enemy aircraft and opened fire with a short 2-second burst at 100 yards. No strikes were observed. I raised my sights slightly, closed to 50 yards and again opened fire with a 2-second burst. The enemy aircraft exploded in mid-air. I flew through the blast of the exploded aircraft and saw the other Me 262 break off to port. I fired two 2-second bursts from the quarter position but did not observe any strikes. I then saw Red

3 (F/O Fraser) attacking from above and to the rear of the second enemy aircraft. Both the enemy aircraft and Red 3 disappeared below cloud, I observed a plume of black smoke bulging above cloud.'

Fraser followed his victim below cloud, and saw it crash into the ground. The two German pilots, *Oberleutnant* Hans-Georg Richter and *Feldwebel* Werner Witzmann, both of II./KG 51, were killed.

Early in March the Me 262 fighter units made their first determined attempt to engage the American bomber formations. On the 3rd there were 29 Me 262 sorties, mainly from III./JG 7, put up against the heavy USAAF attacks on Magdeburg, Brunswick, Hannover, Chemnitz and other targets; twenty of the German pilots reported making contact with the enemy and they claimed the destruction of six bombers and two fighters. *Hauptmann* Heinz Gutmann of III./JG 7 was shot down and killed during the action. The USAAF records list only three bombers and six fighters lost on that day, and there was no claim of a Me 262 destroyed.

Following this great exertion the Me 262 fighter units saw little action for more than two weeks. Then, on the 18th, 37 jet fighters were launched against the heavy attack on Berlin by 1,221 bombers escorted by 632 fighters. During this action the new R4M air-to-air rocket was used for the first time; twelve of these 55 mm impact-fused missiles were carried on a wooden rack under each wing of the Me 262, making 24 rockets in all, in addition to the four 30 mm cannon. *Oberleutnant* Guenther Wegmann of III./JG 7 led six Me 262s carrying R4M against one of the American formations, and the German pilots loosed off their rockets against the B-17s from a range of 1,000 yards.

The victims were the 100th Bomb Group (the Bloody Hundredth), whose B-17s had become badly strung out. Two of the heavy bombers went down right away and a third suffered serious damage. During a subsequent firing pass a third B-17 had its entire tail blown off, and the bomber damaged in the first attack was finished off. Then the jet fighters had to break away to avoid the escorting P-51s, streaking in to protect their charges.

Guenther Wegmann was on his way back to Parchim when he sighted a further formation of B-17s and, after manoeuvring into position, went in to attack with his guns. He opened up at the bomber on the right of the formation and saw hits on the starboard wing. Then accurate return fire from the bombers began to strike home and his Me 262 shuddered under the impact of several hits. He felt a severe blow against his right leg and at the same time his laminated glass windscreen starred under the impact of one of the enemy rounds and his instrument panel was wrecked by another. Wegmann accelerated away from the bombers and their escorts and took stock of his situation. He felt down at his leg and found, to his horror, that one of the .5-in rounds had passed clean through it leaving a hole large enough for him to push in his hand; strangely, however, he felt no pain. His first inclination was to try to get his crippled fighter back to Parchim, though with many of his instruments shot away he had to fly the aircraft 'by the seat of his pants' and control the engines by ear. Then, as he descended past 4,000 m (about 13,000 feet), a tongue of flame came streaming back from his right engine. Now there could be no question of reaching his base at Parchim: he had to bale out before the fire reached his fuel tanks. Wegmann jettisoned his canopy, undid the seat harness, pulled off his helmet and throat microphone and then rammed the control column forwards. The centrifugal forces lifted him out of the cockpit like a cork out of a champagne bottle. The injured pilot came down near Wittenberge, where one of the first to reach him was a red-cross sister who improvised a tourniquet to stop the arterial bleeding. Her move saved Wegmann's life, but there was nothing anyone could do to save his leg; a couple of hours later it was removed in the nearby hospital.

During the action on 18 March 28 German jet fighter pilots reported making contact with the enemy, and claimed the destruction of 12 bombers and one fighter (all except two of the bombers were claimed by JG 7); in fact, probably only eight of the heavy bombers fell to the Me 262s. As well as Wegmann's aircraft, one other Me 262 of III./JG 7 was lost during the action: *Oberleutnant* Karl-Heinz Seeler was seen approaching one of the bomber formations, but then disappeared without trace. Further west, the Ist *Gruppe* based at Kaltenkirchen near Hamburg also lost two Me 262s, in a collision during the scramble take-off

which cost the lives of the fighter ace *Oberleutnant* Hans Waldmann and *Oberfaehnrich* Guenther Schrey.

On the following day, the 19th, the Me 262 fighter units put up 45 sorties; of these 28 made contact with the enemy and claimed six bombers shot down for the loss of two Me 262s and their pilots. On the 20th there were 29 jet fighter missions, of which 24 made contact and nine heavy bombers were claimed for the loss of four Me 262s.

On 21 March the Me 262 units put up 31 sorties against a force of more than a thousand American heavy bombers attacking the airfields at Handorf, Hesepe, Vorden, Zwischenahn, Marx, Wittmundhafen, Ahlhorn, Achmer, Hopsten, Rheine and Essen/Muelheim, most of which were used by the German jets. Twenty-five of the Me 262 pilots reported making contact with the enemy; one was *Leutnant* Fritz Mueller of III./JG 7, who afterwards wrote:

'I took off with my *Rotte* on 21–3–45 against the major enemy incursion in the area Leipzig-Dresden. On this day our radio traffic was especially heavily jammed by the enemy. At 7,500 m, while south of Dresden, I came upon a B-17 flying east at the same altitude as the main bomber force but about 10 km to one side and about 4 km behind it, with four Mustangs above it flying escort. It seemed to me that this machine was on some sort of special mission, and I resolved to attack it. The enemy radio jamming was so powerful that communication was impossible. I flew close underneath the four Mustangs, which were now following my *Rotte* trailing black smoke (which meant they were flying at full throttle); but a glance at my airspeed indicator showed that I would not have to worry about them. The Boeing was now ahead of me in a left hand turn, so that I was flying about 10 degrees to the left and about 5 degrees above it. At about 1,000 m the rear gunner opened up a harassing fire. Then it was all over in seconds. At a range of about 300 m my wing man and I opened up with our cannon and gave it short bursts allowing slight lead. We saw a dozen rounds exploding against the fuselage and between the engines. Then we were already past him. Curving round in a wide circle (with the Mustangs behind us, still trailing smoke but getting smaller the whole time) we observed the end of the bomber. It spun down through about 2,000 m, with several large bits falling from the fuselage and wings, then exploded. At that moment the radio jamming ceased.'

Whatever the mission of the lone B-17 on that

day, it was almost certainly not radio jamming. The sole 8th Air Force unit engaged in that activity was the 36th Bombardment Squadron, which operated B-24s; it put up three aircraft to jam German fighter communications on that day and all returned safely. The most probable explanation of the sudden ending of the radio interference is that the jamming transmitters carried by the 36th B.S. had to be switched off when other American aircraft in the vicinity were using their radar for bombing, lest the transmissions interfered with the blind bombing equipment.

From an examination of the records it seems that five heavy bombers were shot down by Me 262s during this action, compared with a German claim of 13. USAAF fighters claimed the destruction of nine Me 262s, but JG 7 lost only two pilots on that day and I./KG (J) 54 lost one more. The only American combat report that can be linked with specific German losses on that day was from Lieutenant Harry Chapman of the 361st Fighter Group in a P-51D, who was able to make good use of his K-14 gunsight:

'While flying Yorkshire Blue 3 on March 21st approximately 0955 in the vicinity of Dresden, Germany, escorting B-17s, 20,000 feet, my box of bombers was attacked by a flight of 4 Me 262s. After hitting the bombers, they continued their pass into my flight. We broke into them and my flight leader confirmed their identity. The number 4 man of the enemy flight kept turning into us until he was making a head-on pass at me. With a K-14 sight set at 2,400 feet, I put the pip on his canopy and fired a 1 to 1½ second burst from 10 to 20 degrees deflection. I observed strikes on the nose part of the enemy aircraft and the left side from leading edge of the wing forward burst into flames. He passed to the left of me and was seen by other members of my squadron to be smoking and spiraling down. One member of Yorkshire Yellow flight saw him hit the ground and explode.'

The victim was almost certainly one of the two Me 262s of III./JG 7 which crashed in the Dresden area at about this time; the pilots, *Leutnant* Joachim Weber and *Unteroffizier* Kurt Kolbe, were both killed.

By this stage of the war the Luftwaffe had its own equivalent to the Allied K-14 and gyro gunsights: the EZ 42 sight produced by the Askania company. In service, however, the computing mechanism of the EZ 42 proved so unreliable that if it was fitted in the Me 262 the sight graticule was usually fixed so that it functioned in the same way as the old *Revi* sight.

Of the changes to the Me 262 fighter since its introduction into service almost a year earlier, the most important was the fitting of improved Jumo 004 B-series engines; these now had a slightly longer life (nominally 25 hours running time, though they often failed before this), and could tolerate slightly less-careful throttle handling without bursting into flames. Another modification which proved popular with Me 262 pilots was a new control column with a hinged extension, which allowed greater leverage during flight at high speeds (there were, of course, no powered flying controls at this time).

After the action on 21 March there were further pitched battles between Me 262s and American formations daily until the 25th; then followed a lull of four days, before the next great exertion. On 30 March the Luftwaffe put up 31 jet fighters against the heavy attacks by the 8th Air Force against Hamburg, Bremen and Wilhelmshaven. One of the German pilots in action that day was *Leutnant* 'Quax' Schnoerrer of III./JG 7 who, with his wing man *Oberfaehnrich* Viktor Petermann, made contact with a formation of B-17s near Hamburg. Both pilots attacked the bombers and scored hits, but Schnoerrer's Me 262 was hit by return fire from the enemy gunners and had to break away with his port engine flamed out. He curved away in a descending turn to the south-east, looking for a suitable airfield on which to land his crippled aircraft. It was then, however, that a section of four Mustangs spotted him and came bearing down to attack. Unable to fight or to flee, Schnoerrer rolled his Me 262 on to its back, jettisoned the hood, released his seat straps and fell from the cockpit; but as the tail came past he suffered a severe blow against his right leg. The German pilot's parachute opened normally, but his landing was painful in the extreme: in hitting the tail his leg had been badly fractured. Picked up by civilians, he was driven to the nearby hospital at Uelzen.

And always the German jet fighters were vulnerable when they were taking off or landing. On the same day Captain Robert Sargent of the 339th Fighter Group was leading a pair of P-51s escorting the bombers running in to attack Hamburg when:

'I saw two enemy aircraft taking off from Kaltenkirchen airfield. I called them in and we split-essed down on them. Unfortunately due to their camouflage we lost them for a second and when we got down to their level I was able to pick up just one of them. From here on it was easy. My air speed was 430 mph and I estimated his as being about 230 mph. As we closed I gave him a long burst and noticed strikes immediately, the left unit began to pour white smoke and large pieces of the canopy came off. The pilot baled out. We were at 300 feet at this time and the plane dove into the ground and exploded causing a large oil-like fire which went out almost at once. The pilot's chute did not open fully and the last I saw of him was on the ground near the plane with the chute streaming out behind him. Lt Kunz did a splendid job of covering my tail and after the encounter we pulled up and looked for the second jet. But when we sighted him he was going balls out for central Germany and we couldn't overtake him.'

The pilot of the Me 262 Sargent had shot down, *Leutnant* Erich Schulte of I./JG 7, was killed.

The B-17s and B-24s of the US 8th Air Force were the main victims of the attacks by Me 262s, but they were not the only ones. During the closing months of the war Royal Air Force Bomber Command had been mounting powerful daylight attacks on targets in Germany. On 31 March 460 Lancasters and Halifaxes of Nos 1, 6 and 8 Groups set out to attack the U-boat assembly yards at Hamburg. It had been intended that the bombers should pick up their escorts — twelve squadrons of Royal Air Force Mustangs — over Holland. In the event, however, the third wave of bombers

Victory tally on the Me 262 flown by *Oberfeldwebel* **Heinz Arnold of III./JG 7. Arnold's total victory score was 49, of which seven kills were scored while flying the Me 262. He was killed in action on 17 April 1945, flying a different aircraft.**

drawn from No 6 (Canadian) Group was late at the rendezvous point and missed the escorts. Over the target the Mustangs warded off several attempts by Me 262s to attack the first two waves of bombers. But there was no such protection for the third wave and during the sharp encounter that followed 19 bombers were attacked and three Halifaxes and four Lancasters fell in rapid succession. Following the action the German pilots, who belonged to III./JG 7, claimed to have shot down ten Lancasters. The bombers' gunners claimed to have destroyed four of the jet fighters and probably destroyed three more, but in fact none of the Me 262s were lost during this part of the action. The very speed of the jet fighter attacks was something entirely new to most of the RAF bomber crews and the official report on the action afterwards stated:

'The usual technique of the jet-propelled fighters appears to be an approach from astern or the fine quarters, possibly with a preference for slightly above, opening fire at 800–900 yards and closing rapidly to close range. In a few cases, however, fire was not opened until 300–400 yards. Combat reports stated that the closing speed of these fighters is so great that they frequently do not have time to fire more than one burst. More than one rear gunner reports that although he had opened fire at 900–1,000 yards he had only time to fire 200 rounds before the fighter broke away 3–4 seconds later at 30–50 yards, and one stated he was unable to rotate his turret fast enough to obtain strikes on the fighter at this close range though he had opened fire at it at 900 yards ...'

Almost certainly the reference to the jet fighters 'opening fire at 800–900 yards' related to the R4M rocket attacks, which were made from such ranges. The RAF heavy bomber crews, who flew in vics of threes in a loose gaggle rather than the serried formations of the American counterparts, went into their famous 'corkscrew' evasive manoeuvre when they came under fighter attack. This countermeasure, which was something quite new to the Me 262 pilots, probably prevented the bomber losses from being considerably higher.

Altogether there were 38 sorties by the German jet fighters on 31 March and they claimed 17 bombers and one enemy fighter destroyed, for the loss of four Me 262s. At the same time as the RAF bombers were striking at Hamburg, over a thousand American heavy bombers were attacking other targets including Zeitz, Brandenburg, Brunswick and Halle. USAAF Mustangs claimed the destruction of two Me 262s.

By the end of March 1945 the Me 262 had also started to establish its reputation as a potent counter to the previously immune Mosquito bombers of the RAF attacking targets in the Berlin area at night. Soon after its formation, *Kommando Welter* was re-designated the 10th *Staffel* of *Nachjagdgeschwader* 11. Initially the unit had operated from Burg near Magdeburg; but when Allied bombing had made this airfield unusable, operations continued from a nearby stretch of straight *Autobahn*. By 24 January Welter's personal score using the Me 262 by night stood at two four-engined bombers and two Mosquitoes, thus confirming the usefulness of the jet fighter for night operations. By the end of January the first Me 262B two-seat trainers had arrived at Staaken near Berlin for conversion for the specialised night fighter role. These aircraft carried FuG 218 Neptun radar, with the indicator and control units in the operator's position in the rear seat; the fixed radar aerials on the nose cut about 60 kph (about 38 mph) off the maximum speed of the Me 262, but it still had an ample speed margin even over the Mosquito. The first two-seat night fighter began operations in February, but the conversion of these proceeded only slowly and in fact the majority of the Me 262 night operations were flown by single seaters without radar, their pilots depending on the assistance of searchlights to find their targets. Most, if not all, of the thirteen Mosquitoes lost at night in the Berlin area during the first three months of 1945 probably fell to Welter's Me 262s. Welter himself has been credited in some accounts with the destruction of 20 enemy aircraft while flying the Me 262 by night, but this figure is probably on the high side. Certainly other German pilots were also successful in this role. One was *Feldwebel* Karl-Heinz Becker who claimed the destruction of five Mosquitoes at night between 21 and 30 March; in each case these claims link with British losses. Becker's kills were made flying a single-seat Me 262, with no airborne radar.

April 1945 was to see the climax of the actions between the Me 262s and the American raiding forces, for by now as well as JG 7 and

KG (J) 54, Adolf Galland's elite *Jagdverband 44* had started operations from Munich/Riem. The first major action of the month was on the 4th, when just under a thousand heavy bombers struck at the airfields at Parchim, Perleberg, Wesendorf, Fassberg, Hoya, Dedelsdorf and Eggebeck, as well as the U-boat assembly yards at Kiel. By now the American fighter pilots had perfected the art of catching the German jet fighters in the act of taking off and climbing away from their bases, and as the bombers approached Mustangs moved into position over the enemy airfields.

Major Rudolf Sinner of III./JG 7 was climbing away from Parchim through a hole in the cloud to engage the bombers, with seven Me 262s, when he suddenly caught sight of Mustangs diving on his force from out of the sun. Lacking the speed to escape, the Messerschmitts broke formation and dived back for the protection of the flak round their airfield. Sinner's assailants were P-51s from the 339th Fighter Group. Captain Kirke Everson afterwards reported:

'At about 0915 hrs Red Flight dropped below the broken clouds to investigate an airfield at Parchim while the remaining flights circled at 10,000 feet. Several Me 262s came up through the clouds and our squadron immediately dove into them. Lt Croker and I attacked the one nearest to us, who immediately dove into the clouds taking evasive action. When we came out of the cloud he was about 1,600 feet range and 2,000 feet altitude. We fired two more bursts and his right unit caught fire. He again went into another cloud and when he came out we were still on his tail.'

Sinner was now in an almost impossible position. The diving Mustangs were much faster than he was and, because of the proximity of the ground, he could not dive away to gain speed. He could now see eight Mustangs closing in for the kill, and as he made for cloud his fighter received its first hits. Sinner's throttles were fully forward but the jet fighter was gaining speed with almost painful slowness. In an effort to reduce drag and so increase his acceleration the German pilot pressed the firing button for his R4M rockets; but there was a fault in the mechanism and they remained firmly in place. The next thing Sinner knew was that his aircraft was hit again; this time it caught fire and the cabin began to fill with smoke. The German pilot jettisoned his canopy and jumped from the Messerschmitt, which by now was flying at about 700 kph (about 440 mph); he was indeed fortunate to miss the tail of the aircraft, and his parachute opened just before he hit the ground. Suffering burns to the head and hands, Sinner was rushed to hospital.

Leutnant Franz Schall, who had taken off with Sinner from Parchim, was also caught by the Mustangs and shot down during the action; but he managed to parachute to safety.

Messerschmitt Me 262s from other bases did succeed in getting off unmolested, however; and once it had attained fighting speed the jet fighter was as formidable as ever. At about the same time as Sinner came under attack at Parchim, *Leutnant* Fritz Mueller was leading other Me 262s off from Laerz. He easily evaded a force of Thunderbolts sweeping ahead of the bombers, then he caught sight of a formation of Liberators heading south-eastwards from the Bremen area. He closed in rapidly on his quarry, in a descending turn to the right:

'From a range of 600 m I fired off all of my R4M rockets, aiming about 50 m in front of the first Liberator to allow for deflection. They struck the fuselage and wing centre section of one of the Liberators flying in the middle of the formation. It reared up, fell back, then began to go down.'

Mueller watched his victim level out, and it seemed he would have to make a second attack to finish it off:

'But before I could get into firing range, the Liberator began to go down rapidly in a wide descending turn to the left. I saw six parachutes leaving it. Then the Liberator stood on its head and went vertically down from 2,000 m into a cloud bank, in the Bremen area.'

Almost certainly the unit Mueller's *Staffel* had attacked was the 448th Bomb Group, which lost three B-24s in rapid succession to an attack by jet fighters.

According to German records the Luftwaffe put up 47 jet fighter sorties on 4 April; of these 44 reported making contact with the enemy and they claimed the destruction of seven bombers and two fighters and the probable destruction of three bombers. Eight jet fighters were lost and five damaged; five jet pilots were killed or missing, and three wounded.

The German pilots converting on to the Me

Opposite, top: Me 262s coming off the assembly line at the heavily camouflaged factory at Laupheim near Ulm. During the early months of 1945 large numbers of these aircraft were accepted by the Luftwaffe, but only a small proportion of them served with the front-line units. *Selinger*

Opposite, centre: An Me 262 carrying the 'Running Fox' emblem of JG 7 and, unusually for this aircraft, a pair of launching tubes for 210 mm rockets on the bomb racks under the nose. None of the pilots of JG 7 interviewed recall having seen such an installation and it is believed it was a one-off modification which saw little use. *Girbig*

262 during March and April 1945 found themselves pitch-forked into the chaos of the final weeks of the war with no time for any formal training course. One of these was *Leutnant* Walther Hagenah, an experienced fighter pilot with several victories flying the Messerschmitt Bf 109 and the Focke Wulf FW 190. He well remembers the cursory training on the Me 262 he received when he was sent to III./JG 7: 'Our "ground school" lasted one afternoon. We were told of the peculiarities of the jet engine, the danger of flaming out at high altitude, and their poor acceleration at low speeds. The vital importance of handling the throttles carefully was impressed upon us, lest the engines caught fire. But we were not permitted to look inside the cowling at the jet engine itself — we were told they were very secret and we did not need to know about them!' Towards the end of March Hagenah was given one dual flight in an Me 262B trainer, a solo flight in an Me 262, and then he was pronounced ready to fly the single-seater. Since he was undergoing his conversion at an operational unit, however, he was able to fly only when there was an aircraft not needed for combat. There were other problems: 'By the time I reached III./JG 7 there were

Leutnant **Walther Hagenah received a hasty conversion on to the Me 262 at the end of March 1945, and was sent into action with less than six hours on type.** *Hagenah*

insufficient spare parts and insufficient spare engines; there were even occasional shortages of J-2 fuel. I am sure all of these things existed and that production was sufficient, but by that stage of the war the transport system was so chaotic that things often failed to arrive at the front-line units,' he recalled. An experienced pilot with some training in instrument flying, Hagenah was able to cope with the transition to the Me 262 with little difficulty; but around him he saw less-experienced pilots trying to do the same thing, and for them the problems were far greater: 'In our unit, flying the Me 262, we had some pilots with only about a hundred hours total flying time. They were able to take-off and land the aircraft, but I had the definite impression that they were of little use in combat. It was almost a crime to send them into action with so little training. These young men did their best, but they had to pay a heavy price for their lack of experience.'

By the end of the first week in April 1945 more than 1,200 Me 262s had been accepted by the Luftwaffe. On 9 April however only about 200, or one in six, were serving on the strength of the front-line units distributed as follows:

Stab/JG 7 (fighters)	5
I./JG 7 (fighters)	41
III./JG 7 (fighters)	30
Jagdverband 44 (fighters)	about 50
I./KG (J) 54 (ex-bomber pilots flying fighters)	37
10./NJG 11 (night fighters)	about 9
I./KG 51 (fighter-bombers)	15
II./KG 51 (fighters-bombers)	6
NAGr 6 (ex-Kdo Brauegg, reconnaissance)	7

That figure, of 200 Me 262s in service with the front-line units, was probably never exceeded. Of the thousand others that had been accepted, possibly half had been destroyed by enemy action in the air or on the ground, or in accidents. Probably about a hundred served with non-operational units. The remainder sat, unused, in railway sidings or aircraft parks. During the final months of the war the business of getting more than a small proportion of the available Me 262s into action, in the face of the debilitating Allied air attacks on German airfields and the transport system, proved beyond the Luftwaffe.

10 April saw the climax of the Me 262 operations when 55 fighter sorties, the greatest number there would ever be, were put up to counter attacks by more than 1,100 US heavy bombers with strong fighter escort on military targets around Oranienburg and the airfields at Neuruppin, Briest, Zerbst, Burg near Magdeburg, Rechlin, Laerz and Parchim.

One of those taking off to engage the raiders was Walther Hagenah, on his first operational flight in the Me 262. Hagenah took off from Laerz, with an inexperienced young Feldwebel pilot as wing-man; his account of the action gives a vivid insight into the problems faced by the German pilots:

'Once above cloud at about 5,000 m I could see the bomber formation clearly, at about 6,000 m. I was flying at about 550 kph (340 mph) in a shallow climb, and turned towards them. Then, as an experienced fighter pilot, I had that old "tingling on the back of neck" feeling that something was wrong. I scanned the sky and, ahead and high above, I caught sight of six Mustangs passing above from almost head-on. At first I thought they had not seen me, and continued towards the bombers. But to be on the safe side I glanced back and it was a good thing that I did, because the Mustangs were curving round and diving on the pair of us.'

With the Mustangs' increased speed in the dive, and Hagenah's reduced speed in the climb, the former closed in rapidly and opened fire at extreme range. Tracer rounds began to flash past the jet fighters, disconcertingly close.

'I lowered my nose slightly to increase my speed and resolved to try to outrun the Mustangs. I did not attempt any manoeuvres to throw off their aim: I knew that the moment I turned, my speed would fall and then they would have me. I told the Feldwebel with me to keep going, but obviously he was scared of the tracers because I saw him weaving from side to side, then he broke away to the left. That was just what the Mustang pilots wanted and in no time they were on to him. His aircraft received several hits and I saw it go down and crash.'

During all of this the Mustangs had ignored Hagenah. From a safe distance he watched the enemy fighters re-form and turn west for home. Vengefully he went after them.

'I closed on them rapidly from behind, but when I got to about 500 m the Mustang leader started to rock his wings and I knew I had been seen. So I loosed off my 24 R4M rockets, into the middle of them.'

Hagenah felt sure that one or two of his

rockets scored hits on the enemy fighters, but a detailed search of the American records has revealed no mention of this. Keeping his speed high the German pilot curved away from the Mustangs and soon left them far behind him. By now his fuel was beginning to run low so Hagenah made a quick check of his position and found he was near Koethen.

'I called the airfield and said I wanted to land there. They told me to be careful: there were "Indians" (enemy fighters) in the vicinity. When I got there I caught sight of enemy fighters making strafing attacks on the airfield, but the light flak defences were giving them a hard time and I was able to approach unnoticed. Then it seemed that I was spotted, because almost as one the Mustangs started to pull up. Perhaps their leader thought I was bringing in some fighters to engage them. Certainly he did not realise I was alone and short of fuel. I made a tight approach, chopped the throttles and hurled the Messerschmitt down on the grass. Before I could breath a sigh of relief at having got down safely, however, the Mustang leader realised what had happened and they were back again. But fortunately the airfield flak defences were able to beat them off and I was not hit.'

Meanwhile, other Me 262s had been able to get through to the bombers. In hit-and-run attacks on the force of 400-odd B-17s attacking Oranienburg, the jet fighters knocked down five bombers. The 41st Combat Wing reported: 'The formation was attacked by five jet aircraft immediately after bombs away. The planes came in high from 5.30 and 6 o'clock and shot down two aircraft, both flying the No. 2 position in the high element of the Lead and Low Squadrons respectively.' The 94th Combat Wing, part of the same attacking force, reported: 'Attacked just after the target with three to four Me 262s attacking singly in trail. Attacks were made from 5 to 7 o'clock, level and above. The enemy aircraft started their attacks from approx. 1,000 yards out, coming in as close as 50 yards before breaking away to the right of the bomber formation. Enemy pilots seemed very aggressive and daring ...', After the action gunners on board the bombers reported 'These Me 262s had two or three guns in each wing just outside the jet units ...', a clear reference to the use of R4M rockets which were ripple-fired off their underwing racks.

Of the 55 Me 262s which had taken off for this, the strongest-ever reaction by German jet fighters against an American attack, 48 reported making contact with the enemy. Ten heavy bombers were destroyed, against a German claim of nine certainly and three probably destroyed. The American counter-attacks against the jet fighters were both vigorous and effective, however: 27 Me 262s, almost half the number which had taken off, were destroyed; five German pilots were killed and 14 missing. Escorting fighter units claimed a total of 20 Me 262s destroyed, a number which finds general confirmation in the German loss records. Yet even for this, the most powerful jet fighter reaction to an American attack, less than a third of the Me 262s available to the front-line fighter units had got airborne. The losses they inflicted could easily be borne by the attackers, while the losses they suffered on that day came close to one in ten of the operational Me 262 fighter pilots.

The action on 10 April was followed by a rapid decline in the Me 262 operations, for by now the Allied ground forces were advancing deeply into Germany from both the east and the west. On that day Hanover fell, while in the south the spearhead of the American advance was nearing Nuremberg. In the east the Red Army was preparing to cross the Oder, from positions within 100 km (60 miles) of Berlin. This general weakening of the military situation was immediately reflected in the order of battle of the jet fighter units, as the dwindling resources were concentrated on keeping going a few selected *Gruppen*. On 11 April, the day following the climax of the Me 262 operations, I./JG 7 and I./KG (J) 54 were both disbanded; so too were the remaining units with Me 262 fighters flown by ex-bomber pilots, KG (J) 6 and II./KG (J) 54, which had never become operational. The surviving jet fighter units were squeezed into the areas not immediately threatened by the Allied advances: in Schleswig-Holstein and Denmark in the north, and Bavaria, Austria and Czechoslovakia in the south.

For the week that followed, the Me 262s saw relatively little action. Then, on the 19th, they re-asserted their presence in dramatic fashion during a sharp attack on B-17s of the 490th Bomb Group near Prague. First an Me 262 made a head-on pass on the formation and knocked down a bomber from the leading squadron; then two more jets attacked and sent down three more bombers. The attackers belonged to III./JG 7, which had withdrawn to Prague/Ruzyne from its threatened bases in the Berlin area. The jet fighters did not get off scot-free, however, and Mustangs of the 357th Fighter Group claimed seven shot down in the area.

In an effort to provide the Me 262 with the ability to destroy enemy bombers at long range, one aircraft was fitted with a single 50 mm MK 214 high velocity cannon and tested in action. The MK 214, a modified version of a gun designed for installation in German tanks, fired a shell weighing 1.5 kg (3.3 pounds) and had an effective firing range of about 1,000 m (3,300 feet). The rate of fire was 150 rounds per minute and the high explosive shells were heavy enough to destroy the largest bomber with a single hit almost anywhere on the structure. But in operational use the automatic ammunition feed system of the modified tank gun proved over-sensitive to

'G' forces, and frequently jammed. *Major* Willi Herget of *Jagdverband 44*, in charge of the trials, found that the heavy cannon functioned well enough when tested against ground targets. During his two attempts to engage enemy bombers in the Me 262 fitted with the MK 214 however, the gun jammed on both; on the second occasion, while he was struggling to clear the jam, he ventured too close to the bombers he intended to attack and their return fire knocked out one of his engines forcing him to break away. After that the development of the MK 214 for air-to-air use in the Me 262 was dropped, and Herget reverted to a standard version of the jet fighter.

During the final days of April there were sporadic actions by the Me 262 units, but in the face of all-pervading Allied air supremacy they achieved little. One of the few combats of note occurred on 26 April, when *Generalmajor* Adolf Galland led a force of six Me 262s of *Jagdverband 44* off from Munich/Riem to engage enemy bombers in the area. One of the jet

Major **Wilhelm Herget, who flew the Me 262 during its operational trials with the 50 mm cannon, shaking hands with Hitler on 5 May 1944 following the award of the** *Ritterkreuz* **with Oakleaves. Herget later served with** *Jagdverband 44. Herget*

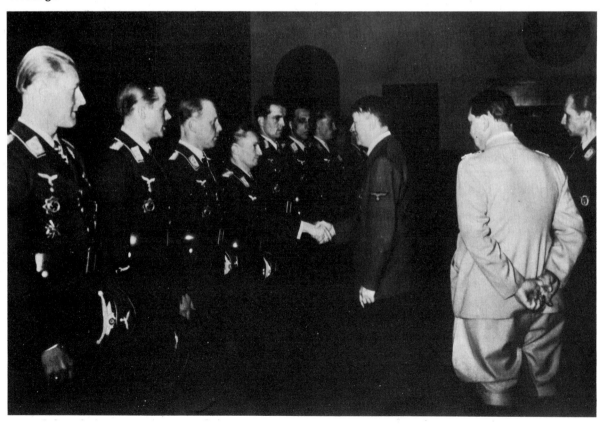

fighters suffered engine trouble early on and had to turn back; the remainder continued with their mission and intercepted the bombers, French-flown B-26 Marauders of the First Tactical Air Force. Meeting the American formation almost head-on, the Me 262s passed over it then wheeled round to attack from the rear. Galland lined up on one of the bombers but, in the heat of the moment, forgot to switch the R4M battery to 'live'; the rockets remained embarrassingly on their rails when he pressed the firing button. The lapse did not save the Marauder, however. Galland closed in to short range and, following an accurate burst with his 30 mm cannon, it blew up. The German pilot pulled his Me 262 round the falling debris, then cngaged a second bomber and saw his rounds exploding against it. Then, as Galland banked away to observe the effect of his attack on the second bomber, his Messerschmitt came under attack from one of the P-47s escorting the Marauders. His assailant was Lieutenant James Finnegan of the 50th Fighter Group, who later wrote:

'I saw two Me 262s "come out of nowhere" and in the flick of an eye literally blow up two bombers. After a moment I saw one of the 262s below me flying in the opposite direction. I turned over on my back, pulled tight on the stick and almost immediately had the enemy aircraft in my sights. I got off two quick bursts but couldn't see if I hit anything because the nose of my aircraft was pulled high to get a good lead. However, I then dropped the nose and observed what I thought were bits and pieces coming from the cowling. In addition, I saw smoke trailing from the wing.'

Finnegan was not mistaken: his rounds had smashed into the instrument panel and engines of the Messerschmitt, and Galland himself received several splinter wounds to his right leg. The German pilot broke off the action and escaped into cloud, then returned to Riem.

The pilots of *Jagdverband 44* claimed to have shot down four of the Marauders, and this is born out by the American records: the 42nd Bomb Wing lost three B-26s which went down immediately, and one more was so seriously damaged that it was forced to crash-land. Captain Robert Clark, also flying a P-47 of the 50th Fighter Group, shot down one of the Me 262s but the German pilot was able to parachute to safety.

The action on 26 April marked the virtual

Lieutenant James Finnegan of the 50th Fighter Group, who shot up Adolf Galland's Me 262 during the action on 26 April 1945. *Finnegan*

end of the Me 262's operational career, as one by one the last of the airfields were overrun by Allied ground forces.

For all of the great hopes entertained for the Messerschmitt 262 earlier in the war, during its nine months of operations it had been able to achieve little. From a detailed study of British and American records it appears that in the fighter role it caused the destruction of no more than 150 Allied aircraft — for the loss of about 100 Me 262s in aerial combat. In the fighter-bomber role its attacks had been so ineffectual that only rarely did they merit even a mention in Allied reports.

There are many reasons for this lack of success, but overshadowing all else is the fact that only a very small proportion of the Me 262s built ever went into action. After the end of October 1944 the various Messerschmitt plants were turning out Me 262s in numbers far greater than the Luftwaffe could usefully employ; and by the end of the war more than 1,400 had been delivered. Yet there were never more than about 200 in service with operational units at any one time; and rarely, if ever, were more than 60 Me 262 sorties of all types — fighter, fighter-bomber, night-fighter and reconnaissance — mounted on any one day. The chaotic supply situation in Germany during the final six months of the war, resulting from the incessant Allied air attacks on the German transport system, imposed a severe brake on every stage of the Me 262 operations.

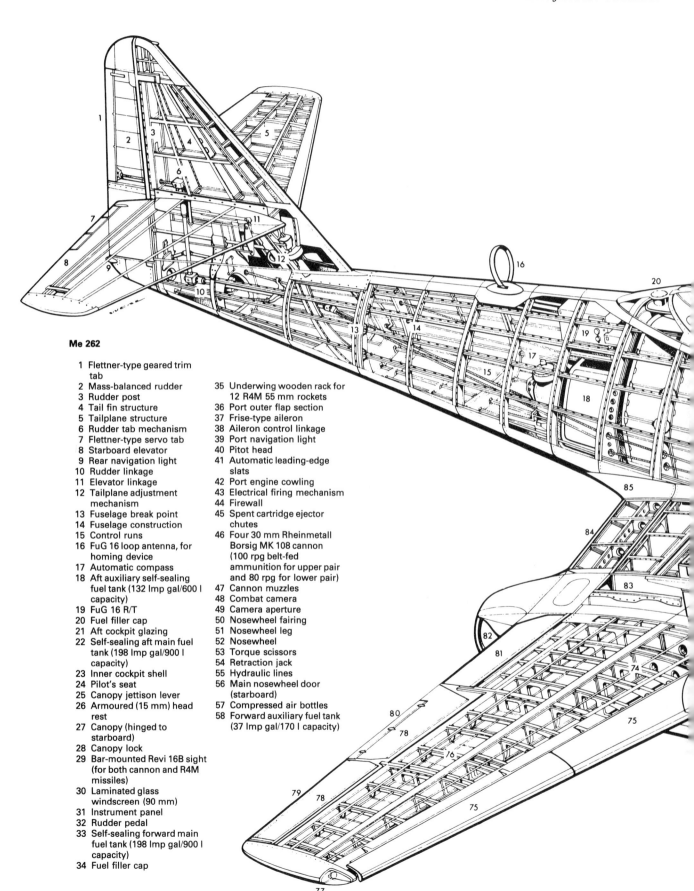

Me 262

1 Flettner-type geared trim
   tab
2 Mass-balanced rudder
3 Rudder post
4 Tail fin structure
5 Tailplane structure
6 Rudder tab mechanism
7 Flettner-type servo tab
8 Starboard elevator
9 Rear navigation light
10 Rudder linkage
11 Elevator linkage
12 Tailplane adjustment
   mechanism
13 Fuselage break point
14 Fuselage construction
15 Control runs
16 FuG 16 loop antenna, for
   homing device
17 Automatic compass
18 Aft auxiliary self-sealing
   fuel tank (132 Imp gal/600 l
   capacity)
19 FuG 16 R/T
20 Fuel filler cap
21 Aft cockpit glazing
22 Self-sealing aft main fuel
   tank (198 Imp gal/900 l
   capacity)
23 Inner cockpit shell
24 Pilot's seat
25 Canopy jettison lever
26 Armoured (15 mm) head
   rest
27 Canopy (hinged to
   starboard)
28 Canopy lock
29 Bar-mounted Revi 16B sight
   (for both cannon and R4M
   missiles)
30 Laminated glass
   windscreen (90 mm)
31 Instrument panel
32 Rudder pedal
33 Self-sealing forward main
   fuel tank (198 Imp gal/900 l
   capacity)
34 Fuel filler cap

35 Underwing wooden rack for
   12 R4M 55 mm rockets
36 Port outer flap section
37 Frise-type aileron
38 Aileron control linkage
39 Port navigation light
40 Pitot head
41 Automatic leading-edge
   slats
42 Port engine cowling
43 Electrical firing mechanism
44 Firewall
45 Spent cartridge ejector
   chutes
46 Four 30 mm Rheinmetall
   Borsig MK 108 cannon
   (100 rpg belt-fed
   ammunition for upper pair
   and 80 rpg for lower pair)
47 Cannon muzzles
48 Combat camera
49 Camera aperture
50 Nosewheel fairing
51 Nosewheel leg
52 Nosewheel
53 Torque scissors
54 Retraction jack
55 Hydraulic lines
56 Main nosewheel door
   (starboard)
57 Compressed air bottles
58 Forward auxiliary fuel tank
   (37 Imp gal/170 l capacity)

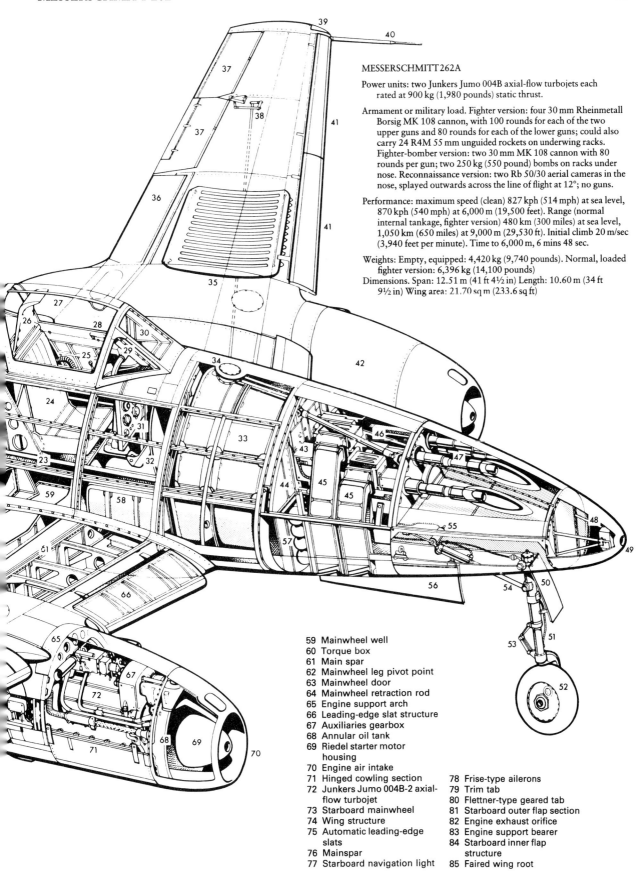

MESSERSCHMITT 262A

Power units: two Junkers Jumo 004B axial-flow turbojets each
    rated at 900 kg (1,980 pounds) static thrust.

Armament or military load. Fighter version: four 30 mm Rheinmetall
    Borsig MK 108 cannon, with 100 rounds for each of the two
    upper guns and 80 rounds for each of the lower guns; could also
    carry 24 R4M 55 mm unguided rockets on underwing racks.
    Fighter-bomber version: two 30 mm MK 108 cannon with 80
    rounds per gun; two 250 kg (550 pound) bombs on racks under
    nose. Reconnaissance version: two Rb 50/30 aerial cameras in the
    nose, splayed outwards across the line of flight at 12°; no guns.

Performance: maximum speed (clean) 827 kph (514 mph) at sea level,
    870 kph (540 mph) at 6,000 m (19,500 feet). Range (normal
    internal tankage, fighter version) 480 km (300 miles) at sea level,
    1,050 km (650 miles) at 9,000 m (29,530 ft). Initial climb 20 m/sec
    (3,940 feet per minute). Time to 6,000 m, 6 mins 48 sec.

Weights: Empty, equipped, 4,420 kg (9,740 pounds). Normal, loaded
    fighter version: 6,396 kg (14,100 pounds)
Dimensions. Span: 12.51 m (41 ft 4½ in) Length: 10.60 m (34 ft
    9½ in) Wing area: 21.70 sq m (233.6 sq ft)

59 Mainwheel well
60 Torque box
61 Main spar
62 Mainwheel leg pivot point
63 Mainwheel door
64 Mainwheel retraction rod
65 Engine support arch
66 Leading-edge slat structure
67 Auxiliaries gearbox
68 Annular oil tank
69 Riedel starter motor
    housing
70 Engine air intake
71 Hinged cowling section
72 Junkers Jumo 004B-2 axial-
    flow turbojet
73 Starboard mainwheel
74 Wing structure
75 Automatic leading-edge
    slats
76 Mainspar
77 Starboard navigation light

78 Frise-type ailerons
79 Trim tab
80 Flettner-type geared tab
81 Starboard outer flap section
82 Engine exhaust orifice
83 Engine support bearer
84 Starboard inner flap
    structure
85 Faired wing root

In spite of what many others have said, the authors feel that Hitler's insistence that the Me 262 should be used initially as a fighter-bomber, to counter the seaborne invasion of France in its initial stages, was not misplaced. Given a touch-and-go situation such as actually occurred on Omaha beach on D-day, when the invaders were held up on the beaches for several hours and suffered severe casualties, there can be little doubt that a few score of resolutely handled jet fighter-bombers attacking the troops coming ashore might have tipped the balance and forced the landings to be abandoned. Nor did Hitler's order delay the introduction of the fighter version into action by much. Due to the difficulties experienced with getting the Jumo 004 engine into mass production, the Me 262 did not start to become available in quantity until October 1944; and by then Hitler's order for it to be used only as a fighter-bomber had been rescinded. In the event the order delayed the operational deployment of the first Me 262 fighter *Gruppe — Kommando Nowotny* — by less than six weeks.

Certainly the Messerschmitt 262 was the finest all-round fighter in service in any air force at the end of the Second World War. Yet its margin of effectiveness over the best fighters in the opposing air forces, and in particular the Mustang, was not great enough to redress the gross numerical inferiority of the Luftwaffe during the closing stages of the war.

Appendix

THE ME 262 AS A COMBAT AIRCRAFT

After the war Allied Intelligence officers conducted a detailed questioning of several German pilots who had flown the Me 262 in action. The resultant report, entitled 'The Me 262 as a Combat Aircraft', gave a fascinating insight both into the technical features of the aircraft itself and the way it was used in action. The section that follows is based closely on that report.

TECHNICAL FEATURES OF THE ME 262

Modified Control Stick

At speeds of about 800 kph (500 mph) the ailerons and elevators of the Me 262 became very difficult to move with the normal control column. A new type of control column was therefore developed, to give an increased mechanical advantage to offset this difficulty; this was installed in later production aircraft. The control column itself was fitted with an extendable section, which could be locked in place to give a greater leverage.

Gyroscopic Gunsight — EZ 42

The EZ 42 gyroscopic gunsight was fitted in several aircraft of JV 44, but faulty installation made the sight useless and it was locked so as to function in the same way as the old fixed-graticule reflector sight.

Automatic Throttle Control

On the Me 262s in service the throttles had to be advanced slowly up to 6,000 rpm to avoid burning out the jet units. Above 6,000 rpm the throttles could be pushed all the way forward at once, because an automatic fuel flow and pressure regulator prevented a too sudden increase in the amount of fuel entering the jets and a resultant overheating. By the end of the war a new regulator had been developed to control the fuel flow, so that the throttles could be set at any point and the new regulator would ensure a safe and gradual acceleration of the engine to the rpm selected. Just before the war ended the new regulator had been tested and found satisfactory.

Rocket-Assisted Take-off

Many experiments had been conducted into rocket-assisted take-offs with the Me 262; two 500 kg (1,100 pound) thrust rockets shortened the take-off run, without bombs or rocket projectiles, by between 250 and 300 m (820–980 feet). Take-offs with two 1,100 kg (2,200 pound) thrust rockets had been made in as little as 400 m (1,300 feet), without bombs or rocket projectiles.

Performance Calculator

The endurance and speed of the Me 262 was dependent on such variables as air temperature, barometric pressure and weight. To assist pilots in calculating this a special circular slide rule was produced by the Messerschmitt Company and issued to operational units.

New Type Parachutes

The great speed of the Me 262 made it dangerous to bale out with an ordinary parachute, because if the pilot pulled the ripcord immediately on clearing the aircraft the sudden deceleration might damage both parachute and pilot. So two new types of parachute were developed. One type was fitted with metal rings to hold the shroud lines together in pairs just below the canopy, thereby reducing the circumference of the canopy and lessening its immediate effect. Once the initial shock of opening had been absorbed, the rings slid down the shroud lines and allowed the parachute to develop normally.

The other type was the so-called 'strip parachute' (*Baenderfallschirm*), in which the canopy was made out of spaced circular strips of silk instead of continuous pieces. It opened more slowly and the rate of descent was more rapid than with the normal type of parachute. This type was soon discarded, however, because the pilots were most vulnerable during take-off and landing and therefore needed a parachute that would deploy rapidly if they had to bale out at low altitude.

Flying Qualities

Because of the range of speeds over which the Me 262 could operate — 250 to 950 kph (156 to 590 mph) — the design was a compromise and it could not turn as sharply as the more conventional fighters of the period. Acceleration and deceleration in level flight were accomplished relatively more slowly in the Me 262 than in earlier fighters, but the clean airframe and the absence of an airscrew enabled the Me 262 to dive very fast.

At speeds between 950 and 1,000 kph (590 and 621 mph) the airflow around the fighter approached the speed of sound and the control surfaces no longer influenced the direction of flight; the result varied from aircraft to aircraft: some dropped a wing and went into a dive, while others went into a steadily steepening dive. Vertical dives were not performed in the Me 262, because it exceeded its limiting Mach number too rapidly.

Because of the great speed range of the

aircraft and its great fuel consumption with the resultant unbalancing, constant trimming was necessary during flight as speed changed and fuel was consumed.

Take-off and Landing Distances

Distances for take-off varied considerably with air temperature and pressure, but the following figures were given for an Me 262 with full fuel load and 24 × R4M rockets:

Grass field   1,800–2,000 m (5,900–6,600 feet)
Concrete runway
                         1,500–1,800 m (4,900–5,900 feet)

Minimum landing distance with fuel almost expended and no rocket projectiles was 1,100 m (3,600 feet) on either a concrete runway of a grass field.

Service Ceiling

Altitudes as high as 11,850 m (about 38,500 feet) had been reached by the Me 262 during test flights, but the operational ceiling for formations of Me 262s was set at 9,250 m (about 30,000 feet) because of the difficulty of holding formation at higher altitudes and the likelihood that the jet engines would flame out at altitudes much above this. Any throttle movement at altitudes above about 6,000 m (about 20,000 feet) was liable to cause a flame-out of the engine involved.

Servicing

The Jumo 004 jet unit fitted to the Me 262 was supposed to last from 25 to 35 hours, but in practice they lasted only about ten hours' flying time. The prescribed time for changing and checking a unit was three hours, but in actual practice it took eight to nine hours because of poorly fitting parts and the lack of trained staff.

Fuelling the aircraft could be accomplished in eight to 15 minutes under operational conditions, depending on the pumping speed of the refuelling vehicle.

Operation on One Engine

The Me 262 functioned efficiently on one jet unit, and speeds of 450 to 500 kph (280 to 310 mph) for as long as 2¼ hours had been attained. In attempting such flights an altitude of about 7,700 m (25,000 feet) had first to be reached before one of the engines was flamed out, and the aircraft had to descend to below 3,000 m (about 10,000 feet) to restart it. Landing with one unit shut down was possible, but it was regarded as a hazard to be avoided if at all possible.

Armament

The standard armament of the Me 262 was four 30 mm MK 108s. The close grouping of the guns in the nose was considered ballistically ideal, but some trouble was experienced in firing in the turn, when the centrifugal forces sometime tore the ammunition belts; this fault was later curied by altering the feed mechanism. The guns were adjusted to converge their fire on a point between 400 and 500 m (1,300 and 1,650 feet) ahead of the aircraft.

In combat against enemy bombers, the Me 262s of JV 44 carried 24 × R4M rocket projectiles, twelve under each wing. Each projectile contained 500 g (1.1 pound) of Hexogen and had a considerable blast effect. The rockets were ripple-fired, and diverged to cover an area the diameter of the wingspan of a four-engined bomber at 600 m. Several victories were achieved with R4M and it was planned to install as many as 48 under the wings of the Me 262 for even greater effect. The trajectory of the R4M was almost the same as that of the MK 108 cannon, so the ordinary gun sight could be used to aim it.

TACTICAL EMPLOYMENT ON THE ME 262

The Me 262 was employed as a fighter, fighter-bomber, shallow dive bomber and for reconnaissance.

Employment of the Me 262 by JV 44 to attack USAAF bombers

In January 1945, by special permission of Goering, a new Me 262 fighter unit was formed at Brandenburg-Briest by *Generaleutnant* Galland, formerly chief of the Inspectorate of the Fighter Arm. This unit, known as *Jagdverband 44* or *Jagdverband Galland*, trained with units of JG 7 at Briest until late March, then it moved to Munich-Riem where it became operational. The 40 to 50 pilots of the unit included Galland himself, about ten holders of the *Ritterkreuz*, a dozen other highly experienced pilots and twenty-odd new pilots who had shown some promise. JV 44 was operational throughout April 1945 from Riem and moved in the last days of the war to Salzburg-Maxglan, where it was overrun by American troops on 3 May.

During the short time they were operational, Galland and his more experienced pilots developed some concept of how the Me 262 should best be used in combat. They carried through a number of attacks on Allied bomber formations and achieved some success, despite heavy losses inflicted by the overpowering fighter escort that constantly harried them.

Rarely were more than 16 aircraft of JV 44 serviceable for any one mission, with the result that during any attack on USAAF bombers the German force was far outnumbered by the American fighter escort. The primary mission of the jet aircraft was to attack and destroy the bombers, and combat with Allied fighters was not accepted unless unavoidable. Hence, all the tactical employment of the Me 262 in JV 44 was hampered by numerical inferiority and strict limitation of the combat objective.

The large turning radius and poor acceleration of the Me 262 made the *Kette* (element of three aircraft) instead of the *Schwarm* (element of four aircraft) the most practical basic formation; however, JG 7 did fly missions in elements of four. The element of three was chosen by JV 44 because the lack of manoeuvrability of the jet rendered it difficult for a larger element to

stay together in aerial manoeuvres. When turns were made, the formation had to be held by cutting inside or overshooting rather than by use of the throttles. When shifting position in a turn, the two rear aircraft in the element of three tried to pass below the leading aircraft to avoid losing sight of it, since downward visibility was poor in the Me 262.

The use of the element of three as the basic formation was dictated by yet another consideration: as a result of the great speeds reached by the aircraft at low altitude and because of its relatively short endurance, assembly after take-off was more difficult to effect than with piston-engined fighter aircraft. Hence it was necessary for each element to take-off simultaneously, and the standard German airfield runways were just wide enough to permit the take-off of three Me 262s side by side.

When attacking bombers formations of *Staffel* size, about nine aircraft flying in three elements of three, were used. On the approach flight the formation was made up of one element leading and the other two on the flanks slightly higher and farther back. The interval between aircraft in each element was about 100 m (330 feet) in the climb and 150 m (500 feet) in level flight. The interval between elements was about 300 m (1,000 feet). If the formation was made up of more than one *Staffel*, the other *Staffeln* flew on the sides of the leader slightly higher, or were strung out to one side in echelon. Because of the great speed

The loose *Kette* three-aircraft element used by *Jagdverband 44*, drawn to scale.

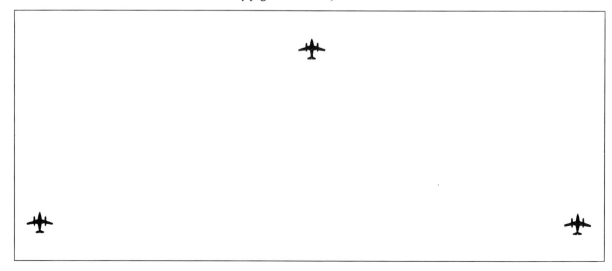

of the Me 262 no top cover was required against Allied fighter attacks.

The jet formations were directed on to the Allied bomber formations by ground controllers using radar. Once the bomber formation had been sighted the jet fighters manoeuvred to attack one of the groups of bombers from the rear. Getting into position for this was often difficult because of the great speed and large turning radius of the jet aircraft, and decisions had to be made early while the bomber formation was some way away. The great distances involved made it difficult to judge the altitude and course of the bombers at this time, further complicating the problem.

For maximum effect it was considered advisable for one *Staffel* to attack each bomber group. In the case of a multi-*Staffel* formation, the *Staffeln* would separate and attack separate groups. The approach flight was best begun from a distance of 4,500 m (5,000 yds) behind the bomber formation with an altitude advantage of about 2,000 m (2,200 yds), but entry into the bomber stream could be accomplished

from as little as 2,000 m behind the bombers.

The Me 262s formed into a column of three *Ketten* and dived to a position about 500 m (550 yds) below and 1,500 m (1,650 yds) behind the bombers to gain speed, and then pulled up and flew straight and level for the last 1,000 m (1,100 yds). The purpose of the dive was to increase speed to about 850 kph (530 mph), necessary on account of the Allied fighter escort which was almost certain to be closing in to engage; for the best marksmanship, however, a somewhat lower speed would have been desirable. It was considered essential for the jet fighters to hold their formation and attack the whole width of the enemy bomber group, in order to split up the defensive fire from the bombers' guns.

The aircraft of JV 44 used the ordinary reflector sight, but they had painted on its screen two lines spaced so as to frame the wingspan of a B-17 at 650 m (710 yds). At this point the twenty-four R4M rocket projectiles under the wings were fired at the bomber chosen as target. Fire was then opened with the

The type of attack described in the report, in which the pilot pulled up sharply at the end of his dive to 'dump' speed before going into his attacking run. This type of attack was known to American bomber crews as the 'Roller-coaster' or the 'Leap frog'.

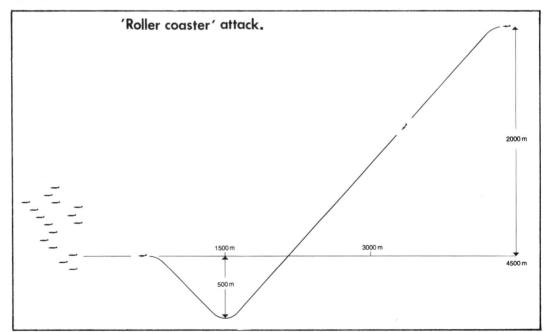

four 30 mm MK 108 cannon. The pilots aimed at the general shape of the bomber, since the range was too great to aim at any particular part of it.

In practice it was found difficult to manoeuvre into position exactly behind the bomber in the time available, and if there was any deviation the fighter pilot had to aim his rounds in front of the target.

The three *Ketten* in column would attack the bomber group, closing the range to about 150 m (160 yds), at which point they began their get-away. Because of the great speed of the Me 262 they did not have to break away behind or inside the bomber formation but could pass through or above it, thus avoiding exposing their bellies in curving away to one side. The best get-away route was found to be a flat climb passing as close as possible above the top elements of the bomber formation so as to make it difficult for the bombers gunners to score hits. Passing under the bombers was regarded as unwise because pieces of debris from damaged bombers may be sucked into the jet units and damage them.

After passing through or over the bomber formation, the Me 262s could either break off their attack and fly back to their base, or repeat the attack on another formation further ahead. If they decided to break away, a shallow dive enabled them to gain enough speed to outdistance the fastest Allied fighters.

If the Me 262s had ammunition left they could pass on to the next bomber group ahead and attack it in a similar manner. But if too much speed had been lost in the first attack, the second was rendered perilous by the Allied fighter escort which by this time would usually be in position to dive to attack from above.

Reassembly of the Me 262s was not usually effected after the attack, because the elements had become too widely dispersed and fuel would be running low. The elements returned home alone, relying on their speed to outrun the Allied fighters.

Head-on attacks occurred on a few occasions by accident, and it was found that the closing speed of the jet aircraft and the bombers was too great to permit accurate sighting and firing, and there was no possibility of observing hits.

German pilots were of the opinion that the Me 262 would have been an effective weapon

against the USAAF daylight raids over Germany if mass employment had been possible. But the gross numerical inferiority, the fuel shortage and the lack of good pilots prevented adequate combat testing of the potentialities of the Me 262.

Use of the Me 262 to combat Allied fighters and fighter-bombers

The use of the Me 262 as an attack fighter against Allied bombers was dictated by the impossibility of using other German fighters for this purpose and by the need to do something to stop or hinder the Allied raids. But the German pilots regarded the ideal role of the Me 262 to be that of a pure fighter, finding and destroying Allied fighters and fighter-bombers. They were sure that the employment of a few hundred jet aircraft against the Allied fighter escorts would have forced the Allied air forces to use jets themselves or drastically to curtail their operations over Germany in daytime.

The two principal advantages of the Me 262 as a fighter were its speed and climbing ability; it was admittedly inferior to Allied piston-engined fighters in turning and close manoeuvring. The two paramount qualities of speed and climb could always be used, it was felt, to gain the two basic advantages which decide aerial combat, namely surprise and superior altitude. Operating at normal altitudes for fighter combat a formation of Me 262s could, upon sighting Allied fighters, accept or refuse combat as the German formation leader chose. He could climb to gain altitude and at the same time overhaul any Allied formation. When attacked from above the Allied fighter pilots showed excellent discipline and turned into the attacking jets; but sometimes stragglers could be shot down, and the Me 262s could then pull up and repeat the attack.

Some Me 262s were lost when they attempted to 'dog fight' with Allied fighters, especially with P-51 Mustangs. In such cases the German pilots made the mistake of losing speed to gain manoeuvrability, and the P-51s proved still more manoeuvrable. If the Allied fighters were circling defensively it was considered practical to dive and fire while going through a one-third or half turn with them, then climb away. Longer turning engagements always put the Me 262 at a disadvantage.

When Me 262s were themselves attacked

from above at a range too close to permit them to turn into the attacking Allied fighters, the jets had only to go into a shallow dive, put some distance between themselves and the Allied fighters, then turn round and engage. If the attack was from the same altitude and behind, instead of from above, the Me 262s could easily climb away from their assailants.

In engaging Allied fighter-bombers flying at 5,000 m (about 16,000 feet) or lower, the Me 262s enjoyed an even greater advantage than against ordinary Allied fighters. The speed advantage of the Me 262 over ordinary fighters was most marked lower down, and in addition to this the fighter-bombers were slowed by their armour and bombs. The speed of the Me 262 enabled it to fly low so as to sight the Allied fighter bombers silhouetted against the higher clouds, then climb and attack from underneath; such tactics were not feasible for piston-engined fighters.

The Me 262s engaged Allied fighters only on rare occasions, when combat with bomber formations was not possible. But the German pilots regarded the correct use of the Me 262 to be that of attacking the Allied fighter escort and keeping it occupied, thereby leaving the bombers as easy prey for the German piston-engined fighters. In the event, however, by the time the Me 262 units were ready for combat the supplies of fuel were so short that the High Command had to order all fighters to concentrate on engaging the enemy bombers.

Use of the Me 262 as a shallow-dive bomber and a ground strafing aircraft

When used by KG 51 the Me 262 carried a bomb load of one 500 kg (1,100 pound) or two 250 kg bombs and the bombing results were as accurate as those obtained with the Fw 190. The high speed of the aircraft made it possible for it to operate at low altitudes despite the Allied air superiority. When first operational, however, the Me 262s of KG 51 were forbidden to fly lower than 4,000 m (13,000 feet) over Allied-held territory to prevent their falling into enemy hands; this resulted in very inaccurate bombing.

Shallow-dive attacks were carried out by formations of four Me 262s, flying in line abreast at about 4,600 m (15,000 feet) or lower with about 100 m (330 feet) lateral interval between aircraft. The target was

approached from a slightly oblique angle and, when it disappeared under the right or the left engine nacelle, the pilots pulled round into 30° shallow dives using the ordinary reflector sight for aiming. During the dive a speed of between 850 and 900 kph (530 to 560 mph) was reached; to prevent it rising further the pilot would throttle back the engines to 6,000 rpm and, if necessary, ease back on the stick. Bombs were released at altitudes around 1,000 m (3,250 feet). At the time of bomb release it was essential that the rear fuel tank had already been emptied, otherwise the sudden change in trim to tail heavy could cause the nose to rise up abruptly and the wings might break off. Several Me 262s and pilots had been lost in combat to this cause.

The Me 262 had been used on several occasions for ground strafing attacks against advancing Allied troops, though German pilots did not feel that it was really suitable for this purpose. The MK 108 cannon had so low a muzzle velocity that attacks had to be carried out from 400 m (1,300 feet) or below if they were to be accurate; and the ammunition load of 360 rounds was too little for this purpose. Furthermore, the Me 262 carried insufficient armour to protect the pilot from enemy ground fire.

Line-up of nine Me 262s at Lechfeld in June 1945, prior to their move to Melun in France where German aircraft were collected before shipment to the USA. *Smithsonian Institution*

The Me 262 armed with the 50 mm MK 214 cannon being readied for its ferry flight to Melun, France, before shipment to the USA. *Smithsonian Institution*

Left, top: Me 262 reconnaissance aircraft at Melun. Just beneath the camera bulge on the side of the nose, can be seen the camera window on the underside of the fuselage. *Smithsonian Institution*

Left, below: Close-up of the MK 214 50 mm cannon-armed Me 262 christened 'Wilma Jeanne' by US forces, being readied for the flight to Melun. *Smithsonian Institution*

Below: An Me 262B two-seat trainer being towed to its dispersal point at Melun. *Smithsonian Institution*

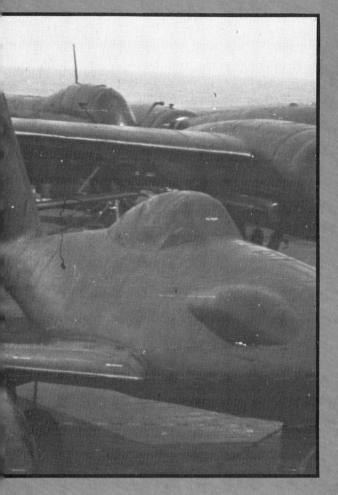

Left and opposite below: Without doubt the most unusual collection of aircraft ever parked on the deck of an aircraft carrier! When the Royal Navy escort carrier HMS *Reaper* left Cherbourg on 20 July 1945 for Newark, New Jersey, she carried an assortment of 38 captured German aircraft for testing in the USA. There were 12 Me 262s (four ordinary fighters, one fighter with a 50 mm cannon, three Me 262B trainers, one Me 262B night fighter and three photographic reconnaissance aircraft), 2 Arado Ar 234s, 3 Heinkel He 219s, 2 Dornier Do 335s, 9 Focke Wulf Fw 190s, a Tank Ta 152, 3 Messerschmitt Bf 109s, a Messerschmitt Bf 108, a Junkers Ju 88, a Junkers Ju 388, 2 Flettner Fl 282 helicopters and a Doblhoff jet helicopter. All of the aircraft parked on the deck have been cocooned to protect them from the effects of salt spray during the voyage. *Smithsonian Institution*

Below: One of the Me 262s brought to the USA on HMS *Reaper*, given the serial number T-2-4012, was passed to Hughes Aircraft for high speed testing. The armament was removed and the gun ports covered over, the gaps in the airframe were sealed to remove all unnecessary drag, then several coats of high gloss paint were applied to give the aircraft a smooth finish. The resultant aircraft had a performance considerably better than the Lockheed P-80, the fastest US jet aircraft at that time. According to unconfirmed reports, at one stage Howard Hughes expressed the wish to pit his aquisition against the P-80 in one of the Bendix and Thompson Jet Trophy races; there is little doubt the Me 262 would have won. But, again according to unconfirmed reports, General 'Hap' Arnold got to hear of the proposal and squashed it firmly. *Smithsonian Institution*

Above and right: Close-up of the crew's accommodation
in the night fighter version.

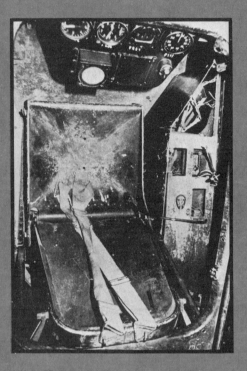

The radar operator's instrument panel, showing
the British climb-and-descent, altimeter, compass and
airspeed indicators and the single screen for the Neptun
radar.

The pilot's instrument panel in the night fighter.
This particular aircraft carries several British
instruments installed at Farnborough, including a climb
and descent indicator and altimeter reading in feet, and
an airspeed indicator reading in miles per hour.

The port side of the radar operator's position, showing
the simple control unit for the Neptun radar and the
voltmeter.

This Me 262, one of the three tested by the French Air Force, suffered a double engine failure during a flight on 6 September 1945. The pilot, *Commandant* (now General Housset, made a skilful belly landing near Tousson causing minimal damage to the aircraft, which was subsequently repaired and flown again. *EC Armées*

Above: One of three Me 262B night fighters tested by the Royal Air Force at Farnborough.

Below: One of a dozen Me 262s assembled and flown in Czechoslovakia after the war, by the Avia company using components left in the country after the war.

Arado 234

The Arado Ar 234, the world's first true jet bomber, was one of the great white hopes of the Luftwaffe during the final year of the war. Here at last was a machine able to outrun the fastest enemy interceptor and penetrate the strongest defences. Had the war continued past the summer of 1945 it was planned to equip the major part of the German bomber force with this type. But it was not to be. When the end came only 210 of these aircraft had been built; and such was the general chaos in Germany during the opening months of 1945 that less than half of these ever reached operational units.

Yet although the Arado Ar 234 is remembered principally for being the world's first true jet bomber to go into action, the type was conceived initially as a reconnaissance aircraft; it was in this role that it first went into operation and it was in this role that it achieved complete success.

Work on the new jet reconnaissance aircraft for the Luftwaffe began early in 1941 under Professor Walter Blume, the director of the Arado company, at the firm's Brandenburg plant. The project, initially designated the E 370, took shape as a clean high-winged monoplane with two Jumo 004 turbojets slung under the wings in pods; the projected all-up weight of the aircraft was about 8,000 kg (17,640 pounds). Apart from the new type of propulsion, the only unconventional feature of the E 370 was the method of taking-off and landing: it was to take-off from a wheeled trolley which was then released, and land on retractable skids. The German Air Ministry wanted its new reconnaissance aircraft to have a range of 2,150 km (1,340 miles) and, by deleting from the structure the weight and bulk of a conventional wheeled undercarriage the necessary fuel could be carried without resort to a large airframe. Calculated performance figures for the new aircraft were: maximum speed 776 kph at 6,000 m (485 mph at 20,000 feet), an operating altitude of over 11,000 m (35,750 feet) and a maximum range, excluding reserves, of about 2,000 km (1,250 miles). Already the range was slightly down on the original Luftwaffe specification, but the design was accepted and two prototypes were ordered under the designation Arado 234.

By the end of 1941 the airframes of the two prototypes were virtually complete — but then

began the wait for the engines for, like BMW, Junkers had run into difficulties with its new turbojet. Not until February 1943 did Arado receive a pair of 004s, and even then they were pre-production models suitable only for static ground running and taxi-ing trials.

In the late spring of 1943 a pair of flight-cleared Jumo 004s finally became available and the Arado 234 made its maiden flight on 30 July from Rheine near Muenster, with Flight Captain Selle at the controls. The flight passed off without incident for the aircraft, though there was a problem with the take-off trolley: after its release from about 60 m (200 feet) the retarding parachutes failed to deploy properly, with the result that the trolley smashed into the ground and was wrecked. A replacement trolley was rushed to Rheine for the second flight, but it too was destroyed when the parachutes again failed to open after its release. Thereafter the trolley was released immediately the aircraft reached flying speed, and seldom left the ground.

By the end of September 1943 three further prototypes of the Ar 234 had flown and testing was being pushed forwards at the highest priority. Already the new aircraft had aroused considerable interest, not only for the reconnaissance role but also as a bomber. The aircraft had been discussed for this role even before its first flight, during a conference at the

The first prototype Arado 234. *Transit Films*

German Air Ministry on 9 July presided over by Erhard Milch. *Oberst* Peltz, the Inspector of Bombers, had expressed misgivings about the heavy losses suffered by his units at the hands of the continually strengthening Allied defences.

MILCH (jokingly): Now we come to the matter of jet bombers. Peltz is always modest, now he has issued a small demand for a couple of hundred, and he wishes to have them by November at the latest!

PELTZ: December!

OBERST PASEWALDT (a member of Milch's staff): Here we have the Arado 234, on which work is now in progress on the first twenty in the initial production batch of a hundred. The type has not yet flown. When is it going to?

FRIEBEL (representing the Arado company): In one week.

PASEWALDT: The Arado 234 has made a good impression. We await [the flight trials of] this machine, to see if our hopes will be realised. It should be remembered, however, that the Arado 234 has been developed as a reconnaissance aircraft. Its consideration for use as a bomber has been a recent development.

Because it was such a small aircraft, there could be no question of the Ar 234 carrying its bomb load internally; and the use of the trolley for take-off precluded the carriage of bombs under the engines or the fuselage. Accordingly, the Air Ministry placed an order for two prototypes of a new version, the Arado Ar 234B, fitted with a more conventional tricycle undercarriage retracting into the fuselage.

The test programme gradually gained in momentum, though there was a set-back on 2 October when Flight Captain Selle was killed when the second prototype crashed during a test flight. Engineer Hoffmann of the Arado company explained the circumstances of the crash to Milch at a production conference in Berlin three days later:

'The purpose of the test flight was to make an ascent to determine the rate of climb. This ascent was completed at 8,950 m [29,000 feet]. At every 1,000 m Flight Captain Selle reported the temperature and pressure. Then the port engine failed. He went into a glide from 8,950 m to 4,500 m [14,600 feet] at an indicated airspeed of 300 kph [about 190 mph] and experienced elevator vibration at this speed. He noted that the skids, which he now wished to extend, failed to operate at 4,400 m. Then the airspeed indicator failed. He reported all of this by radio, so that it could be written down. He then extended the skids manually and asked to be informed if they were out: he could not tell this from the cockpit, as the indicator had failed. At 1,500 m [4,900 feet] he reported that the port engine had flamed out; he tried to restart it ...One and a half minutes later he reported shuddering and vibration from the elevators and ailerons. Through binoculars it was then possible to see that the port engine was on fire ...'

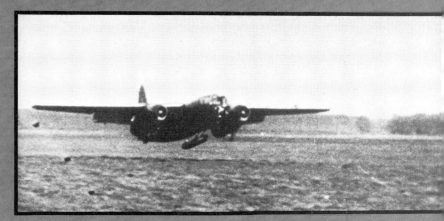

Left: Arado 234 trolley take-off. Following the wrecking of the take-off trolleys during the first two flights, when they were released from too high an altitude, during subsequent flights the trolley was released as the aircraft was about to get airborne and so hardly left the ground. Immediately the aircraft had lifted clear, the braking parachute started to deploy. *Transit Films*

Right, top to bottom: Skid landing sequence by one of the early Arado 234s. *Transit Films*

With one wing down, the aircraft slid straight into the ground from 1,200 m (about 4,000 feet). From a subsequent examination of the wreckage Arado engineers found that there had been a fire inside the wing from the time Selle had first reported the engine failure. The pitot tube to the airspeed indicator ran past the engine, as did the push rods to the ailerons and the landing skids; the fire had caused the partial or complete failure of these systems. The burning engine had broken away from the wing shortly before the aircraft struck the ground, with Selle still on board.

While work proceeded on the wheeled Arados, four further trolley-mounted aircraft flew during December 1943 and the early months of 1944: the 5th and 7th prototypes, similar to the earlier machines; the 6th prototype, fitted with four 800 kg (1,760 pound) thrust BMW 003 turbojets in separate pods under the wing; and the 8th prototype with four BMW 003s paired in underwing pods.

To enable the aircraft to take off fully loaded from short runways when there was little or no wind, the third prototype and subsequent twin-engined aircraft had provision for the installation of a Walter 109–500 liquid fuelled rocket booster pod under each outer wing section. Each pod developed 500 kg (1,100 pounds) of additional thrust for take-off and, complete with sufficient hydrogen peroxide and sodium permanganate for about 30 seconds' running, weighed 280 kg (616 pounds). Once the aircraft was airborne and the rockets' fuel exhausted, the pods were released and parachuted to earth and could be re-used. A system of interconnected electrical pressure switches ensured that if one of the pods failed to deliver thrust, that on the opposite side shut down also thereby preventing a dangerous asymetric thrust condition.

In March 1944 the ninth prototype Ar 234 took the air, the first B version with a built-in undercarriage. Even before it had flown, however, the factory at Alt Loennewitz in Saxony was tooling-up for the mass production of this version. Intended for either the bomber or the reconnaissance role, the Ar 234B was powered by two 900 kg (1,980 thrust) Jumo 004B engines and weighed 5,210 kg (11,464 pounds) empty and 8,427 kg (18,580 pounds) loaded. It had a maximum speed, clean, of 737 kph (461 mph) at 6,000 m (20,000 feet).

Left: The second prototype Ar 234 (circled), crashing in flames after an engine fire on 1 October 1943. Flight Captain Selle was killed in this accident. *Transit Films*

Left, centre: After each flight the Ar 234A had to be jacked up where it had come to rest. The take-off trolley was then manoeuvred into place underneath it, the aircraft was lowered on to the trolley and towed away. *Transit Films*

Below: The eighth prototype Ar 234, with four BMW 003 engines in two paired pods. *via Heise*

Bottom: The ninth prototype Ar 234, the first B version fitted with a retractable wheeled undercarriage, made its first flight in March 1944. This was also the first to be able to carry a bomb load and in this photograph it carries a single SC 1000 (2,200 lb) bomb under the fuselage, and an empty bomb rack under the port engine nacelle. *Smithsonian Institution*

Bottom left: The ninth prototype taxiing out for a heavy-weight take-off with rocket assistance, carrying an SC 500 bomb under each engine nacelle and an SC 250 under the fuselage, making a total bombload of 1250 kg (2750 lb). *Transit Films*

The maximum bomb load was 1,500 kg (3,300 pounds) carried externally. When it carried bombs or drop tanks, the maximum speed of the Arado was reduced by 55 to 80 kph (35 to 50 mph). Range depended on altitude since, speed for speed, the jet engines consumed roughly three times as much fuel at sea level as at 10,000 m (32,500 feet); at 10,000 m the aircraft, clean, had a range of about 1,600 km (1,000 miles), reducing to about 550 km (340 miles) if it remained at low altitude. In practice this meant that the bomber version had an effective operating radius of action, carrying a 500 kg (1,100 pounds) bomb one way and allowing reasonable fuel reserves, of about 480 km (300 miles) for high altitude attacks and about 190 km (120 miles) if the aircraft remained at low altitude. Operating in the reconnaissance role at high altitude with two 300 litre (66 Imp gal) drop tanks, it had a radius of action of about 720 km (450 miles).

Three modes of bombing attack were possible with the Ar 234B: the shallow dive attack, the horizontal attack from low altitude and the horizontal attack from high altitude. The shallow dive attack was the most used method and typically it involved a nose-down throttled-back descent from 5,000 m (16,250 feet) to 1,400 m (4,500 feet), during which the pilot sighted his bombs using the periscopic sight protruding from the top of his cabin. The low altitude horizontal attack was a rather inaccurate method, employed only when poor visibility or low cloud at the target precluded any other method. The pilot simply ran over his target and released the bombs by eye.

Technically the most interesting mode of

attack performed by the Arado was that from high altitude flying horizontally. Using normal map-reading or radio navigational methods, the pilot would take his aircraft to a point about 30 km (about 20 miles) short of the target. He would then engage the Patin three-axis autopilot and swing his control column out of the way to his right. This done, he loosened his shoulder straps and leaned forward to the bomb aiming position, over the eyepiece of the Lotfe bombsight. The bombsight's controls were connected to the aircraft's automatic pilot via a simple form of computer. All the pilot had to do was hold the graticule of the bombsight over the target; the bombsight then fed the appropriate signals via the computer to the autopilot and thus it 'flew' the aircraft through its bombing run. When the aircraft reached the bomb release position, the bombs were released automatically. The pilot then straightened himself up in his seat, tightened his shoulder straps, retrieved the control column, switched out the autopilot and turned the aircraft round for home. All in all, it was a remarkably advanced system for an aircraft of 1944 vintage.

A further innovation with the Ar 234B was the braking parachute to shorten the landing run; it was the first aircraft in the world to have this as a standard fitting.

Early in June 1944, less than a year after the Arado 234A had made its maiden flight, the first of the twenty pre-production Ar 234Bs was completed.

Also in June 1944, the 5th and 7th prototypes were fitted with cameras and issued to the 1st *Staffel* of the Luftwaffe High Command Trials Detachment* at Oranienburg, a special reconnaissance unit which operated under the direct control of the High Command. *Oberleutnant* Horst Goetz took charge of the aircraft and he and another pilot, *Leutnant* Erich Sommer, began training with the new aircraft in readiness for operations. Sommer remembers having little trouble with the trolley method of take-off; it was important to line up accurately on the runway before starting the run, however, because at the lower speeds the lateral control was poor. When it reached

about 160 kph (100 mph) the aircraft's nose began to lift by itself and he pulled the lever to release the trolley; relieved of its 600 kg (1,325 pounds) weight, the Arado would lift cleanly into the air. After the aircraft had landed on its skids, jacking up and refitting the trolley took about 20 minutes, then the Arado could be towed away. During one of the early flights Goetz got airborne but found he was unable to release the trolley. After orbiting the airfield to burn off fuel, he skilfully put the Arado down on the runway at Oranienburg, using almost its full length before he brought the aircraft to a halt.

Goetz's Ar 234s were each fitted with a pair of Rb 50/30 cameras in the rear fuselage. Fitted with 50 cm telephoto lenses, the cameras pointed downwards and were splayed sidewards away from each other at 12 degrees to the vertical across the line of flight. From an altitude of 10,000 m (32,500 feet) this split-pair camera arrangement took in a swathe of ground just over 10 km (6 miles) wide along the aircraft's track.

While Goetz and Sommer learned to handle the two Arados in an operational role, the Allied troops had established themselves ashore in Normandy. Luftwaffe reconnaissance units attempting to photograph the landing areas suffered heavy losses from the screens of enemy fighters, and frequently failed to get through to their targets. German army commanders were left in almost complete ignorance of what was going on behind the front line, and often the first indication of an impending attack was the preparatory bombardment.

To overcome this deficiency, Goetz received orders to move his detachment to Juvincourt near Reims in France for reconnaissance operations. From the start, however, there were problems. On 25 July the two Arados took off from Oranienburg, but Goetz's aircraft suffered an engine failure and he had to turn back. Sommer continued on and landed at Juvincourt without incident. After he landed, his aircraft was hoisted on to a low-loading trailer and towed into a hangar. There the world's most advanced reconnaissance aircraft had to remain, unusable, until its take-off trolley arrived from Oranienburg by rail. It was over a week before the trucks carrying the trolley, the special jacks and other ground

* *Versuchsstaffel der Oberkommando der Luftwaffe*

Top: Trial loading of ground equipment for the Ar 234As of Horst Goetz's *Kommando*, on to a Junkers Ju 352 at Oranienburg in July 1944. Two of the three lifting jacks can be seen, as can two take-off trolleys with the main wheels removed for loading. Horst Goetz was directing the work, wearing his officer's cap and leather flying jacket. When the *Kommando* moved to Juvincourt in France for operations later in the month, however, no aircraft was available and the ground equipment had to go by rail. *Goetz*

Above, left: *Oberleutnant* Horst Goetz commanded the special trials detachment at Oranienburg, which was to carry out the world's first jet reconnaissance missions using the Ar 234. *Goetz*

Above, right: *Leutnant* Erich Sommer, who flew the Ar 234A during the world's first jet reconnaissance mission on 2 August 1944 described in the text. *Sommer*

equipment, spares and rocket pods, were shunted into the railway siding at Juvincourt.

Finally, on the morning of 2 August, everything was ready for Sommer to take-off for the world's first jet reconnaissance mission. The Ar 234, with its rocket pods fitted, was towed out to the main east-west runway. Sommer boarded it, strapped in, completed his pre-take-off checks and started the jet engines. Satisfied that everything was functioning as it should, he released the brakes and pushed open his throttles. Slowly the Arado gathered speed. After a run of about 200 m he pressed the button to fire the booster rockets and Sommer felt a reassuring push against his back as the acceleration increased. Gradually the aircraft became lighter on the ground and, when the pilot released the trolley, the Arado leapt into the air trailing smoke from its boosters. A quarter of a minute after lift-off the rockets, their fuel exhausted, ceased giving thrust. Sommer pushed the button to release them and they tumbled away, then their parachutes opened to lower them gently to the ground.

Sommer established his aircraft in the climb at 13 m per second (2,500 feet per minute) with an initial forward speed of 410 kph (256 mph). Since he had taken off in a westerly direction, he needed only a slight change in heading to point the aircraft for the target area.

As the Arado climbed higher and entered the thinner air, its speed gradually increased.

It took Sommer about 20 minutes to climb to 10,500 m (34,000 feet), by which time the Arado was almost over the battle area. From time to time he jinked the aircraft and glanced behind to see whether there were any condensation trails which might give away his position to enemy fighters; there were none. High over the Cherbourg Peninsula he turned the aircraft on to an easterly heading, easing down the nose and descending about 500 m (1,700 feet) to build up his speed to about 740 kph (460 mph). Then he levelled off and concentrated on flying exactly straight and level for his photographic run. Already the doors protecting the camera lenses were open; now the German pilot flicked the switch to set the cameras running, the automatic mechanism taking one picture with every 11 seconds.

It was a beautifully clear summer day, with scarcely a cloud in the sky. From Sommer's vantage point there was hardly a sign of the life-and-death struggle going on far below. If any enemy fighters did attempt to catch the high-flying Arado, he never noticed them. He was too busy holding his aircraft on a ruler-straight track, so that his cameras could take in the greatest possible area on the limited amount of film in the aircraft's magazines. The first photographic run, taking in the coastal strip, lasted about ten minutes. Sommer then turned through a semi-circle and levelled out, heading westwards for the second run parallel to the first and about 10 km (6 miles) inland. The second run completed, he turned back on to an easterly heading and flew a third run 10 km further inland and parallel to the previous two. Almost at the end of the third run the counters on his camera panel clicked to zero, indicating that he had run out of film.

His mission complete, Sommer continued heading east; now his sole aim was to get back to base with the precious film. Keeping a wary eye open for Allied fighters, he returned to

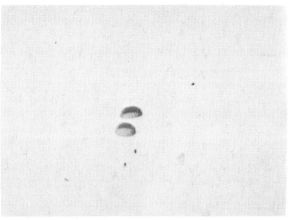

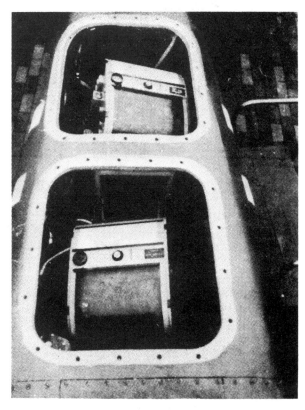

Top: Arado 234 reconnaissance aircraft shortly after taking off, with the rocket pods still in place . . .

Right: Close up of the rear fuselage with the upper camera hatches removed, showing the two Rb 50/30 aerial cameras.

Centre: . . . and the two pods parachuting to earth after release. *Goetz*

Opposite page: Aerial view of the 'Mulberry' artificial harbour off Asnelles sur Mer in Normandy, taken during Erich Sommer's flight on 2 August 1944.

Juvincourt in a high speed descent and set the aircraft down on the grass. Even before the Arado had slid to a standstill on the airfield, men were converging on it from all directions. As Sommer was clambering out, the camera hatch above the rear fuselage had been opened and the magazines of exposed film were being unclipped; then they were rushed away for developing.

During this single sortie, Erich Sommer had been able to achieve more than all of the German reconnaissance units in the west, put together, had done during the past two months: in a flight lasting less than an hour and a half he had photographed almost the entire lodgement area held by the Allies in Normandy. The 380 photographs taken from the Arado caused a considerable stir. By that time the Allies had landed more than 1½ million men, 1½ million tons of supplies and nearly a third of a million vehicles in France. It took a twelve-man team of photographic interpreters

more than two days working flat out to produce an initial report on what the prints showed. The detailed examination of the photographs took weeks. 'After that first sortie, lots of senior officers came to Juvincourt wanting to look over the plane,' Sommer recalled, 'but the whole thing was kept very secret and they were not allowed near it.'

Also on 2 August, Horst Goetz finally arrived at Juvincourt with the other Ar 234. During the three weeks that followed the two aircraft flew thirteen further missions. At last the German field commanders received the regular photographic coverage of the enemy positions which they had craved so long. But the time when such information might have played a decisive part in the land battle was long past. Even as Sommer's initial set of photographs were being scanned by the interpreters, American forces were breaking out of their initial lodgement area and were fanning out into Brittany: the Battle of Normandy was

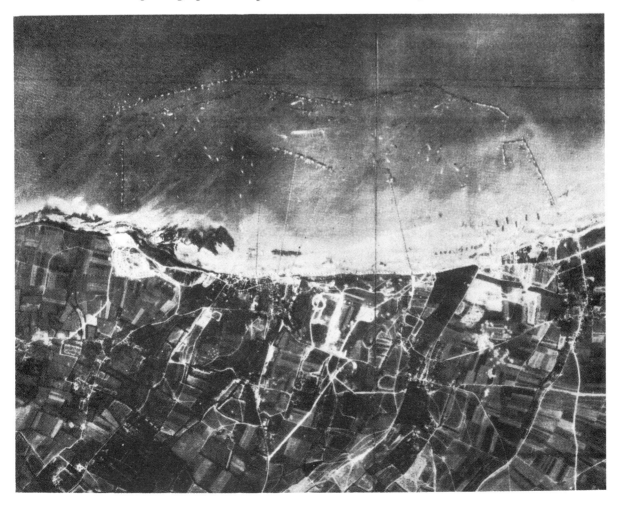

over and the great advance into France was about to begin. The Ar 234s brought back thousands of photographs of the Allied advance, but they did little more than present the German High Command with a minutely detailed picture of a battle already lost.

Like Schenk's Messerschmitt 262s, Goetz's Ar 234s appear to have escaped the notice of the Allied Intelligence services during the Battle of France. It is probably the highest compliment that could have been paid to the high speed reconnaissance machines and their pilots, for their task was to slip in and photograph their targets with a minimum of fuss, then return to base with the precious film.

On 28 August, as the American tanks were nearing Reims, Goetz received orders to move his two Ar 234s from Juvincourt to Chievres. It was then that 'friendly' forces achieved what the Allied fighter pilots could not. As Goetz circled Chievres before landing, the ground defences, who had come to treat almost any aircraft approaching the airfield as hostile, opened fire at him. An accurate shell struck the Ar 234 just beneath the cockpit, knocking out the aircraft's electrical and hydraulic systems. Goetz broke off his approach and found that his flaps and landing skids would not extend. The aircraft was still flyable, however, so he resolved to take it back to Oranienburg where it could receive proper repairs. There Goetz made a skilful flapless belly landing, touching down at about 300 kph (about 190 mph). A few loose stones smashed through the glazed nose and Goetz received some cuts, but otherwise the valuable aircraft came to a halt with remarkably little damage. Goetz had just climbed out of the cockpit, however, when the battered Ar 234 received its coup de grâce: a young fighter pilot taking off from the airfield, not expecting such an obstacle to be in his path, ran straight into the rear of the reconnaissance machine and severed the complete tail with his propeller. Goetz received further injuries from stones and flying glass and was unable to see for a couple of weeks; his Ar 234 was a wreck.

Sommer landed his Ar 234 at Chievres without difficulty, then had to move to Volkel in Holland a few days later as Allied tanks approached the area. Sommer was at Volkel on 3 September, when over 100 Lancaster bombers of the Royal Air Force carried out a heavy

daylight attack on the airfield. Although Volkel's landing ground and camp areas were pot-marked with craters, Sommer's Ar 234 was not damaged in its hangar. The airfield was judged unusable for normal operations so on the following day, 4 September, he made a trolley take-off from one of the taxi-tracks after some of the craters had been filled in. Sommer landed the Ar 234 at Rheine near Osnabrueck, the new base for the jet reconnaissance operations.

The withdrawal to Germany coincided with an end of the missions by the trolley Ar 234s, for by September the improved 'B' version of the aircraft was becoming available with its fitted undercarriage. The slightly wider fuselage necessary to accommodate the undercarriage reduced its speed by about 30 kph (about 20 mph); but still the aircraft was fast enough to avoid fighter interception. There was also some reduction in the radius of action of the aircraft, so two 300 litre (66 Imp gal) drop tanks were carried under the engines for the longer missions. In return for these limitations, of minor tactical importance considering the defensive posture in which Germany now found herself, the Ar 234B was a considerably more flexible machine able to operate from airfields without special ground equipment.

Opposite page: The airfield at Volkel in Holland taken from a Spitfire reconnaissance aircraft of the RAF, after the attack by more than a hundred Lancaster bombers on 3 September 1944. In spite of its pot-marked appearance, the airfield continued in limited use by the Luftwaffe and Erich Sommer took off from there on the day after the attack. His Ar 234 had been in the hangar (circled, A) and was unharmed. He was towed along the taxi way marked with the dotted line and took off down the taxi way shown with the dashed line. The bomb craters along this route had been filled in, then painted so as to appear to the casual aerial observer as though they were still there. This photograph was taken on 6 September; note the aircraft in the process of taking off (circled B). The authors have found no evidence that the Allies discovered the subterfuge.

At Rheine Goetz's unit, now code-named *Kommando Sperling*, gradually built up to a strength of nine Ar 234Bs. Jet reconnaissance missions became a regular feature. Allied fighter patrols over the airfield posed an almost continual problem since, as in the case of the Me 262s, the only time the Ar 234s were vulnerable to fighter attack was when they were flying relatively slowly after take-off and when approaching to land. Goetz had his own system of look-outs posted round the airfield when the Ar 234Bs were operating, to provide warning of enemy aircraft. The jets were towed to the take-off point only when the sky around was clear, then the engines were started and they took off immediately. Goetz's pilots were ordered to keep up their speed as they approached the airfield on their return, and land only on confirmation that there were no enemy fighters about. If there was any danger, the pilots would land at alternative airfields nearby. There were strong flak defences positioned to cover the take-off and landing lanes at Rheine, though Goetz felt that these were never strong enough to deter a really determined enemy.

As well as missions over France, Belgium

**Photographs of Ar 234s of *Kommando Sperling*
engaged in during reconnaissance missions from Rheine,
in the autumn of 1944. Opposite page: Groundcrewmen
pushing out the rocket pod on its special trolley.
Opposite left: Final preparations to the aircraft at the
camouflaged dispersal point. Top: Towing the aircraft
to the take-off point using a refuelling vehicle. Opposite
centre, below and above: At the take-off point the pilot
boarded the aircraft, strapped in and went through the
pre take-off checks. Note the 'Jet-propelled Sparrow
with a Camera' emblem on the nose of the Arado, the
badge of *Kommando Sperling*. Above: Rockets trailing
smoke, the Ar 234 accelerates down the runway.** *Goetz*

**Right: After the mission, the camera magazines were
removed from the aircraft for processing.** *Goetz*

Ar 234B

1 Port elevator hinge
2 Tailplane skinning
3 Port elevator
4 Tab actuating rod
5 Elevator trim tab
6 Geared rudder tab (upper)
7 Rudder hinges
8 Tail navigation light
9 Plywood fin leading edge
10 T-aerial for VHF R/T set
11 Aerial for CBI 3 blind
   approach receiver
12 Aerial matching unit
13 Tailfin structure
14 Rudder construction
15 Rudder post
16 Rudder tab (lower)
17 Lower rudder hinge
18 Rudder actuating rods
19 Parachute cable
20 Cable anchor point/tailskid
21 Starboard elevator tab
22 Elevator construction
23 Tailplane construction
24 Elevator control linkage
25 Tailplane attachment points
26 Elevator rod
27 Port side control runs
28 Internal mass balance
29 Parachute release
   mechanism
30 Main FuG 16 panel
31 Brake parachute container
32 Starboard MG 151 cannon
   muzzle

33 Brake chute door (open)
34 Mauser MG 151/20 cannon
   (rearward firing)
35 Cannon support yoke
36 Spent cartridge chute
37 Access panel (lowered)
38 Ammunition feed chute
39 Tail surface control rods
   (starboard)
40 Ammunition box
41 Bulkhead
42 Fuel vent pipe
43 Fuel pumps
44 Fuel level gauge
45 Rear fuel cell (440 Imp gal —
   2,000 l capacity)
46 Fuselage frames
47 Fuel filler point
48 Fuel lines
49 Inner flap construction
50 Exhaust cone
51 Nacelle support fairing
52 RATO exhaust

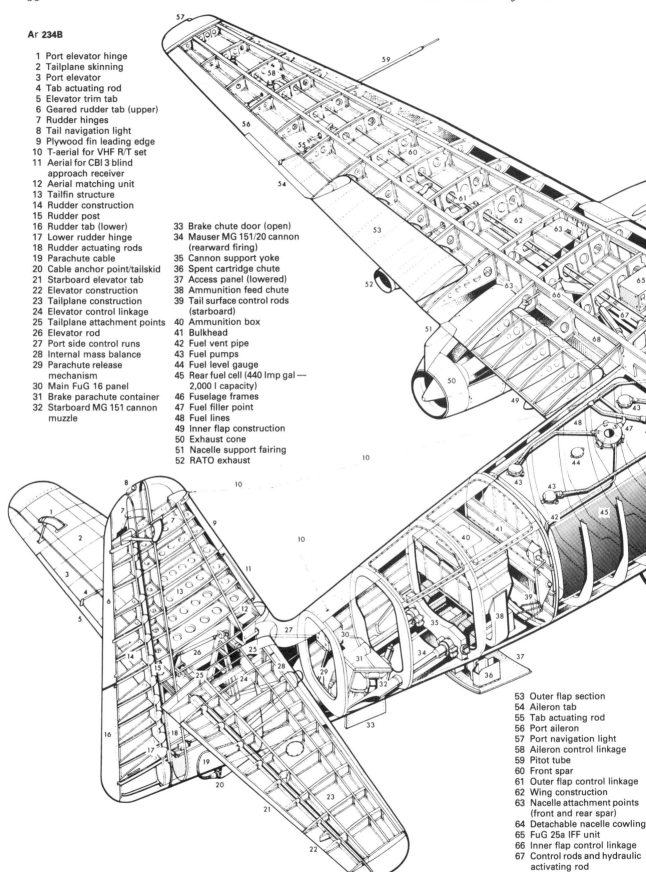

53 Outer flap section
54 Aileron tab
55 Tab actuating rod
56 Port aileron
57 Port navigation light
58 Aileron control linkage
59 Pitot tube
60 Front spar
61 Outer flap control linkage
62 Wing construction
63 Nacelle attachment points
   (front and rear spar)
64 Detachable nacelle cowling
65 FuG 25a IFF unit
66 Inner flap control linkage
67 Control rods and hydraulic
   activating rod

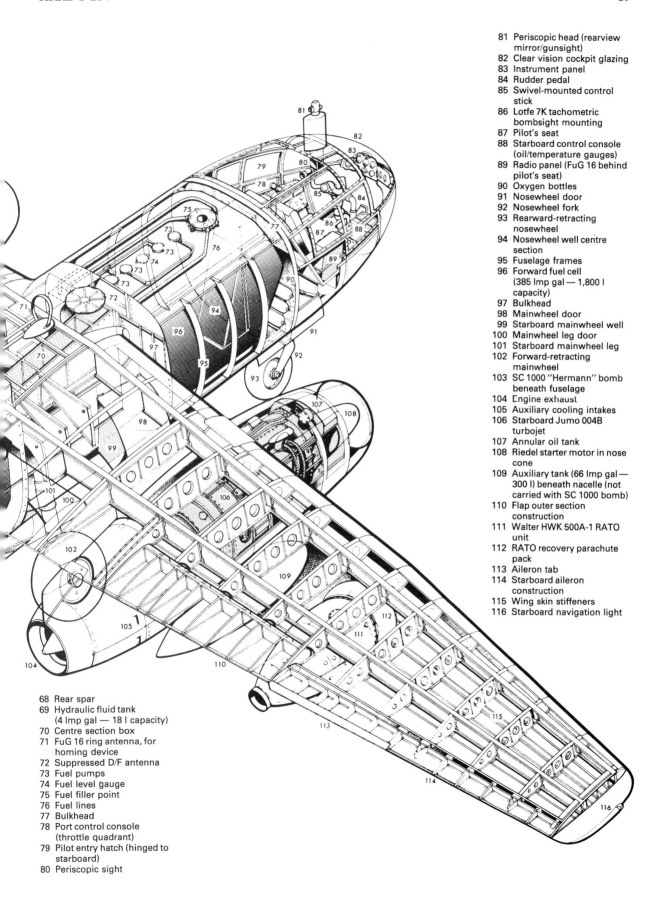

81 Periscopic head (rearview
   mirror/gunsight)
82 Clear vision cockpit glazing
83 Instrument panel
84 Rudder pedal
85 Swivel-mounted control
   stick
86 Lotfe 7K tachometric
   bombsight mounting
87 Pilot's seat
88 Starboard control console
   (oil/temperature gauges)
89 Radio panel (FuG 16 behind
   pilot's seat)
90 Oxygen bottles
91 Nosewheel door
92 Nosewheel fork
93 Rearward-retracting
   nosewheel
94 Nosewheel well centre
   section
95 Fuselage frames
96 Forward fuel cell
   (385 Imp gal — 1,800 l
   capacity)
97 Bulkhead
98 Mainwheel door
99 Starboard mainwheel well
100 Mainwheel leg door
101 Starboard mainwheel leg
102 Forward-retracting
    mainwheel
103 SC 1000 "Hermann" bomb
    beneath fuselage
104 Engine exhaust
105 Auxiliary cooling intakes
106 Starboard Jumo 004B
    turbojet
107 Annular oil tank
108 Riedel starter motor in nose
    cone
109 Auxiliary tank (66 Imp gal —
    300 l) beneath nacelle (not
    carried with SC 1000 bomb)
110 Flap outer section
    construction
111 Walter HWK 500A-1 RATO
    unit
112 RATO recovery parachute
    pack
113 Aileron tab
114 Starboard aileron
    construction
115 Wing skin stiffeners
116 Starboard navigation light

68 Rear spar
69 Hydraulic fluid tank
   (4 Imp gal — 18 l capacity)
70 Centre section box
71 FuG 16 ring antenna, for
   homing device
72 Suppressed D/F antenna
73 Fuel pumps
74 Fuel level gauge
75 Fuel filler point
76 Fuel lines
77 Bulkhead
78 Port control console
   (throttle quadrant)
79 Pilot entry hatch (hinged to
   starboard)
80 Periscopic sight

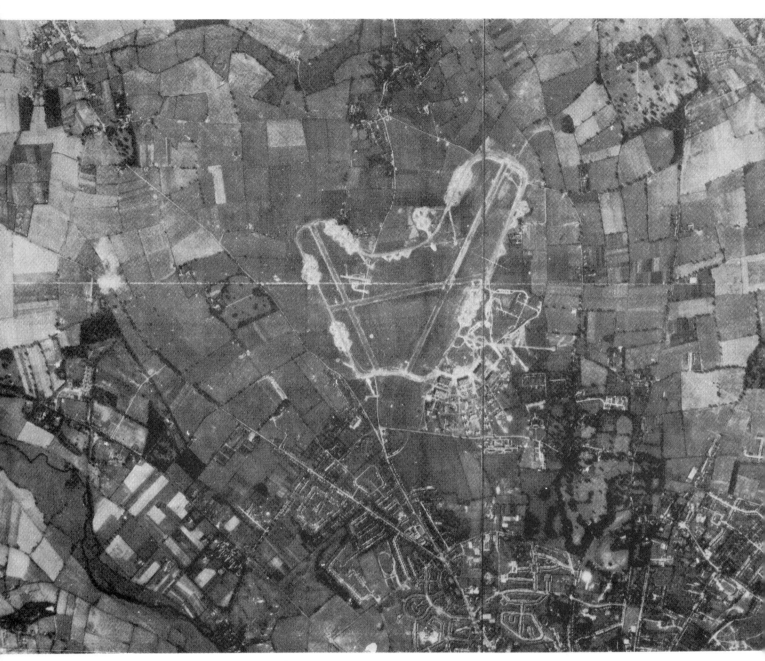

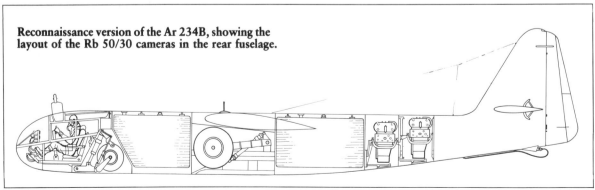

Reconnaissance version of the Ar 234B, showing the layout of the Rb 50/30 cameras in the rear fuselage.

ARADO 234 91

and Holland, *Kommando Sperling* also flew a few sorties over England. On 5 October, for example, Goetz flew a two-hour mission to photograph shipping off the coasts of Norfolk and Lincolnshire. On the following day he took off for a reconnaissance of southern England, only to have a close shave from half a dozen P-47s which arrived over Rheine just after he completed his take-off and released his rocket pods. Fortunately for Goetz, however, the radioed warning of the fighters' approach reached him from the ground observers just in time. The German pilot jettisoned his drop tanks, put down the nose of the Ar 234B to gain speed rapidly, then easily out-distanced the enemy fighters before resuming his climb to altitude. Deprived of the fuel in the drop tanks

Above: For the longer-ranging reconnaissance missions, for example those over England, the Ar 234 carried one 300 litre (66 Imp gal) drop tank under each engine.

Opposite page: The airfield at Horsham St Faith, immediately to the north of Norwich and home of the B-24s of the US 458th Bomb Group, photographed from one of *Kommando Sperling*'s Ar 234s on 11 September 1944.

ARADO 234B

Power units: two Junkers Jumo 004B axial-flow turbojets each rated at 900 kg (1,980 pounds) static thrust.

Armament or military load. Bomber version: usual bomb load carried on operations was a single 500 kg (1,100 pound) bomb or small bomb container under the fuselage; Ar 234s were test flown carrying up to three times this bomb load, but never on operations; normally the Ar 234 bomber carried no gun armament, though a few late production aircraft (like the one in the drawing) carried two fixed rearwards-firing 20 mm Mauser MG 151 cannon with 200 rounds per gun. Reconnaissance version: usually two Rb 50/30 aerial cameras in the rear fuselage, splayed outwards across the line of flight at 12°; no guns.

Performance: maximum speed (clean) 742 kph (461 mph) at 6,000 m (19,500 ft); with 500 kg bomb, 692 kph (430 mph) at 6,000 m. Range at 6,000 m carrying 500 kg bomb, no reserves: 1,560 km (970 miles). Climb to 6,000 m carrying 500 kg bomb, 12 mins 48 secs.

Weights: Empty, equipped, 5,200 kg (11,460 pounds); normally loaded, with two take-off booster rockets and a 500 kg bomb, 9,465 kg (20,870 pounds)

Dimensions: Span 14.4 m (46 ft 3½ in), Length 12.64 m (41 ft 5½ in) Wing area 26.4 sq m (284 sq ft).

Goetz had to cut short this time on reconnaissance, though he was still able to bring back some useful photographs.

Compared with the jet fighter units, *Kommando Sperling* had relatively little trouble with its Jumo 004 engines. The key to extending the life of the early jet engines was careful throttle handling, and the lone reconnaissance aircraft did not require the almost continual speed changes necessary when, for example, fighters flew in formation. Goetz suffered a rare instance of engine failure on 15 November over the North Sea at 10,000 m (32,500 feet) on his way home after photographing airfields in East Anglia. The Ar 234B suddenly began to vibrate uncomfortably. Obviously one of the engines was beginning to play up, but which one? The instruments for both were giving normal indications. Goetz tossed a mental coin and throttled back the starboard engine — wrong! The good engine immediately flamed out, then refused to re-start. The vibration continued, forcing Goetz to shut down the port engine as well. Now he was sitting at the controls of a high speed glider, with an uncomfortably high rate of sink. The aircraft descended to about 2,000 m (6,500 feet) before he was finally able to re-start the starboard engine and returned to Rheine on that one. Afterwards it was discovered that one of the turbine blades had come adrift from the port engine, throwing the whole rotating assembly out of balance.

In spite of the fact that Goetz's reconnaissance Ar 234s had been operating for nearly four months, and he himself had had a brush with enemy fighters six weeks earlier, it was not until 21 November 1944 that Allied fighters first reported seeing an Ar 234 in the air. On that day, as P-51s of the 339th Fighter Group were escorting bombers passing over Holland on their way to targets in Germany, when the Ar 234 hove into view:

'The jet aircraft approached the fighter and bomber formations from the north at an altitude of 27,000 feet which was approximately 1,000 feet above the bomber formation. Jet aircraft passed directly over the formation apparently with power off, indicated airspeed apparently 300 mph. When in 3 o'clock position to our fighter and bomber formation the jet aircraft emitted smoke from each jet nacelle for approximately 10 seconds, increasing the speed of the aircraft as it disappeared into the sun.'

Top: Arado Ar 234Bs of 9./KG 76, photographed at
Burg near Magdeburg late in 1944 when the unit was
working up. *KG 76 Archiv*

Above: An Arado being prepared for a training flight,
with two concrete practice bombs under the starboard
engine bomb rack. *KG 76 Archiv*

Right: Ar 234s being towed out at Burg, prior to a day's
flying. *KG 76 Archiv*

Mock combats carried out at about this time, between an Ar 234B and a Fw 190, highlighted the strong and weak points of the unarmed jet; a report from the Arado company stated:

'The greatest weapon the Ar 234B has over propeller-driven fighters is its speed. In a tight turning fight the Fw 190 could easily get into a firing position. But if the Ar 234B flew straight ahead, or climbed or descended keeping its wings horizontal, it soon outran the Fw 190. If turns have to be made they should be of great radius, that is to say wide turns. One problem is that the vision below and to the rear is restricted, and nothing can be seen rearwards on 30° on either side of the centre line. Due to this limitation of vision it is not possible to detect an attacker coming from directly behind ...'

The report concluded that the FW 190 stood a chance of engaging a correctly-flown Ar 234B only if it could achieve surprise; otherwise the jet aircraft easily evaded it by using its high speed.

Meanwhile, during the closing months of 1944, the IIIrd *Gruppe* of *Kampfgeschwader 76* had been working up with the bomber version of the Ar 234B, at Burg near Magdeburg. On 17 December *Hauptmann* Diether Lukesch, the commander of the 9th *Staffel*, received orders to move forwards a detachment of sixteen aircraft to Muenster-Handorf, and begin operations in support of the German offensive in the Ardennes which had opened the previous day. By the 21st the move was complete. But the bad weather which prevented Allied air operations at this time also prevented those of the Luftwaffe, and the Ar

Hauptmann Diether Lukesch, the commander of the 9th *Staffel* of Kampfgeschwader 76, led the first attack by Arado Ar 234 bombers on 24 December 1944. A week later he led the world's first night attack by jet bombers. *Lukesch*

A mechanic, straddling the engine nacelle as he checks the oil level during the pre-flight inspection, gives scale to the compact Jumo 004 installation. *KG 76 Archiv*

Bottom: Diether Lukesch standing in the cockpit of his Ar 234 as it is towed out for a training flight at Burg ... (below) ... and strapping into the cockpit. *KG 76 Archiv*

234Bs had to remain on the ground for the next two days.

Not until Christmas Eve were the Ar 234B bombers able to go into action for the first time. At 10.14 that morning Lukesch took off from Muenster-Handorf, followed in rapid succession by the remaining eight bombers of the force, bound for Liege. Each Ar 234B carried a single SC 500 (1,100 pound) bomb under the fuselage. The jet bombers, with little to fear from enemy fighters so long as they kept their speed up, flew in a loose trail. After take-off the bombers headed north-eastwards for a few miles to conceal their base airfield in case they ran into enemy aircraft, then turned on to a south-westerly heading for their target and began their climb to a cruising altitude of 4,000 m (13,000 feet). Thirty-five minutes after take-off, Lukesch led the Ar 234Bs in to bomb in a shallow dive attack which took them down to 2,000 m (6,500 feet). The leader released his bomb on a factory complex, the others bombed railway yards in the city; the pilots reported only weak flak defences in the target area. After attacking, the Ar 234Bs remained at 2,000 m and headed straight for

their base at high speed. On his way home Lukesch flew close past a Spitfire which chanced to be in his path. The British pilot, who had no way of knowing that the only gun on board the German jet was the pilot's pistol, banked away sharply and dived to avoid the 'attacker' coming in from behind. All of the Ar 234Bs returned safely to Muenster-Handorf, though one suffered an undercarrige failure on landing and incurred slight damage to the wing; the pilot, *Unterfeldwebel* Winguth, escaped without injury.

During a similar operation against the same target that afternoon, Lukesch led eight Ar 234Bs into the attack and again all returned safely.

On the following day, Christmas, there were two more operations against Liege, both with eight Ar 234Bs. During the morning mission the jet bombers came under attack from

Below: *Major* **Hans-Georg Baetcher (left, in flying jacket) commanded IIIrd** *Gruppe* **of KG 76 early in 1945. Opposite: Climbing into his Ar 234 and strapping in.** *KG 76 Archiv*

Royal Air Force Tempests of No 80 Squadron. Pilot Officer R. Verran managed to close in on one of the Ar 234Bs and claimed strikes on the port engine before he ran out of ammunition. The jet bomber he hit was that flown by *Leutnant* Alfred Frank, which was afterwards wrecked in a crashlanding in Holland; the pilot escaped without injury. During the same mission *Oberfeldwebel* Dierks returned with a failed engine and his aircraft was damaged on landing; once again, the pilot escaped without injury. Returning from the second mission that day *Oberleutnant* Friedrich Fendrich suffered a burst tyre on landing, causing slight damage to the nose of his aircraft.

The *Staffel* suffered its first pilot casualty during an operational mission on the 27th. As he was taking off to attack Allied positions near Neufchateau, *Leutnant* Erich Dick ran into the blast wall of a flak position on the airfield. The aircraft was burnt out in the subsequent fire and Dick was severely wounded.

Operations continued at this rate during the days that followed, whenever the weather permitted. For all of these early missions the Ar 234Bs employed the shallow dive attack tactics similar to those on their initial operation. Lukesch did not favour the high altitude horizontal mode of attack, and never used it during any operational mission that he led. 'During such an attack the pilot could not see behind, and there was a continual worry about being surprised by an enemy fighter; a fighter diving from 1,000 or 2,000 m above could easily reach our speed, especially if we were carrying bombs. Also, flying a straight course for so long would have made things easy for the enemy flak', he recalled. 'The only justification for the high altitude attack would have been to get the extra range; but the targets we bombed were all close enough to our base for us to reach them flying at medium altitudes.'

During the early morning darkness of 1 January 1945, Lukesch led four Ar 234Bs for the world's first night jet bombing mission — though in fact the bombing was intended to deceive the enemy rather than cause damage. The aircraft flew from Muenster-Handorf along a circular route which took them over Rotterdam, Antwerp, Brussels, Liege and Cologne, then back to their base. The primary aim of the mission was to report on the weather over Belgium and Holland in preparation for Operation *Bodenplatte*, the massed attack on Allied airfields by the Luftwaffe planned to open soon after first light. The Ar 234Bs dropped their bombs on Brussels and Liege, to conceal the real object of their mission.

Later that morning Lukesch's deputy, *Oberleutnant* Artur Stark, led six Ar 234Bs to attack the British airfield at Gilze Rijen in Holland. For this operation each of the jet bombers carried a single AB 500 bomb container, loaded with twenty-five SC 15 (33 pound) anti-personnel bombs.

For the rest of January the weather restricted operations severely, and after the first of the month the Ar 234Bs were able to mount attacks on only four other days: on the 2nd, against Liege; on the 14th, against Bastogne; and on the 20th and 24th against Antwerp.

On 10 January 1945 the Luftwaffe Quartermaster General's list recorded only 17 Ar 234Bs in service with operational units, distributed as follows:

9th *Staffel* of *Kampfgeschwader 76*	12
Kommando Sperling (reconnaissance)	4
Kommando Hecht (reconnaissance)	1

By this time the Ist *Gruppe* and the rest of the IIIrd *Gruppe* of KG 76 were re-equipping with the type, though neither unit was to go into action at anything approaching *Gruppe* strength. Even allowing for the aircraft allocated to these units, it is clear that only a relatively small proportion of the 148 Ar 234s delivered to the Luftwaffe by the end of 1944 had in fact been put into service. As in the case of the Me 262s, the rising crescendo of Allied air attacks on the German transport system greatly hindered the formation of operational units with the Ar 234B.

Like the other types of jet aircraft, the Ar 234s were at their most vulnerable during their take-offs and landings. The commander of III./KG 76, *Major* Hans-Georg Baetcher, recalled one occasion when he was returning to his airfield at Achmer to find Allied and German fighters dogfighting overhead '... and the flak gunners, being neutral, firing at everybody!' Short of fuel, Baetcher had no alternative but to run in very fast and make a 'hot' landing. At 400 kph (250 mph) he extended his undercarriage; as soon as his speed fell to 350 kph (220 mph) he lowered his flaps; at 280 kph

(175 mph) he forced the unwilling aircraft down on the runway and immediately streamed his brake parachute. The harsh treatment proved to be too much for the synthetic rubber tyre of the port wheel, which promptly blew out. The aircraft lurched off the runway and Baetcher was treated to a high speed run across the grass before man and machine came to rest shaken, but otherwise little the worse for the experience.

February 1945 saw a reduction in the number of operational sorties by KG 76, as the fuel and other shortages began to bite. Then, in March, came a sudden burst of activity. On the 7th American forces seized the Ludendorf Bridge over the Rhine at Remagen, breaching the Germans' last defensive line along a major natural obstacle in the west. The bridge became a target of the highest priority and *Oberstleutnant* Robert Kowalewski, the commander of KG 76, led several attacks against it. Frequently there was low cloud in the target area, forcing the attacking pilots to employ the low altitude horizontal mode of attack. Bridges are notoriously difficult targets to destroy with conventional bombs and the one at Remagen, though seriously damaged by German demolition charges, survived with powerful anti-aircraft gun protection for ten vitally important days before it finally collapsed. By then, however, the American bridgehead was secure and pontoon bridges had been laid across the river. The final thrust deep into Germany was about to begin. The attacks on the Remagen bridge proved to be the final major effort by KG 76, and from the end of March the unit played little further part in the fighting.

For all of the scares of operating in an environment dominated by enemy air superiority, KG 76 suffered remarkably few casualties however. Between the beginning of October 1944 and 25 March 1945 the authors have found records of only four pilots being lost when the aircraft were shot down by the enemy; over the same period four were killed and seven wounded in flying accidents. It is probable that a few more pilots were lost for whom records cannot be found, but not many.

From September 1944 the reconnaissance Ar 234Bs had operated regularly, photographing Allied positions usually without interference. Early in 1945 Goetz's *Kommando Sperling* had been expanded into a *Staffel*; it

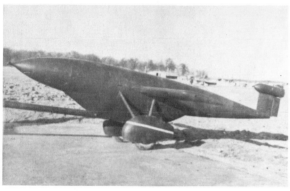

Above: One interesting idea tried out as a means of increasing the radius of action of the Ar 234 bomber was a towed V1 flying bomb, with the warhead, engine and tailplane removed and a wheeled undercarriage fitted, to serve as a container for extra fuel. The trials did not reach an advanced stage.

Major, **later** *Oberstleutnant,* **Robert Kowalewski commanded Kampfgeschwader 76 during the final stages of the conflict and flew several operational missions with the Ar 234.** *Kowalewski*

became the 1st *Staffel* of *Fernaufklaerungsgruppe* (long range reconnaissance *Gruppe*) 123. Two other reconnaissance *Staffeln* re-equipped with the Ar 234B, and were attached to FAGr 100 and FAGr 33. In addition, Erich Sommer had formed his own unit, *Kommando Sommer,* equipped with the Ar 234B and covering the Italian front.

Not until 11 February 1945, after the type had been operating for more than six months, was a reconnaissance Ar 234 shot down by an enemy fighter. On that day Squadron Leader David Fairbanks was leading an armed reconnaissance of eight Tempests of No 274 Squadron RAF when he spotted a lone jet aircraft which he took to be an Me 262. After a lengthy chase the machine was caught and shot down, as it slowed to make its landing approach at Rheine. In fact it was an Ar 234B of Goetz's unit piloted by *Hauptmann* Hans Felden, who was returning after a photographic mission over the port of Hull; Felden was killed when his aircraft smashed into the ground.

Erich Sommer's *Kommando* based at Udine in Italy suffered its only pilot loss on 11 April. *Leutnant* Guenther Gniesmer was engaged in a lone reconnaissance mission when, near Bologna, he had the bad luck to run into a force of bombers escorted by P-51s of the 52nd Fighter Group. Lieutenants Hall and Cooper succeeded in getting into firing positions, and shot him down. Gniesmer baled out of the Ar 234B, but was hit by the tailplane and severely injured. He parachuted into no-man's land and was picked up by German troops, but died in hospital a couple of days later.

In addition to the bombing and reconnaissance missions, early in 1945 a few Ar 234Bs were modified for use as night fighters. These aircraft carried the FuG 218 *Neptun* radar, with nose-mounted aerials; the radar operator sat in an improvised position, inside the rear fuselage aft of the wing. The Ar 234B night fighter carried an armament of two 20 mm MG 151 cannon, housed in a pack mounted under the fuselage. Initially, this ad hoc night fighter unit was commanded by *Hauptmann* Bisping, who lost his life in a crash, and then taken over by *Hauptmann* Kurt Bonow. Late in March 1945, a couple of these provisional Ar 234B night fighters were operated by *Kommando Bonow*. The Ar 234B was clearly under-armed for the bomber-destroyer role, however, and there appears to be no record of it achieving any victories as a night fighter.

On 10 April 1945, the last date for which figures exist, a mere 38 Ar 234Bs were listed as being in service with operational units, distributed as follows:

BOMBER UNITS	
Stab Kampfgeschwader 76	2
6th *Staffel*	5
IIIrd *Gruppe*	5
RECONNAISSANCE	
1st *Staffel Fernaufklaerungsgruppe* 33	7
1st *Staffel Fernaufklaerungsgruppe* 100	6
1st *Staffel Fernaufklaerungsgruppe* 123	8
Kommando Sommer	3
NIGHT FIGHTING	
Kommando Bonow	2

During the closing stages of the war the Arado 234C, powered by four 800 kg (1,760 pounds) thrust BMW 003 engines, was on the point of entering large scale production. With its extra thrust, this version could take-off fully laden from the shorter airfields without the assistance of rockets. Peter Kappus, a civilian test pilot with BMW who flew the Ar 234C, recalled 'The four-engined Ar 234C had a very high performance in the take-off and the climb, but it could not be flown at full power horizon-

The four-engined Arado 234C was on the point of entering service when the approach of Red Army ground forces brought an end to production at Alt Loennewitz. The increased power from the BMW 003 engines greatly improved the bomber's performance, though even at the end of the war this engine was still not reliable.

tally because at the very high speeds it reached it had structural flutter problems.' Even by 1945, however, the development problems of the BMW 003 had not been fully resolved (it will be remembered that at one time this engine was to have powered the Me 262). Kappus had a very lucky escape on 29 March 1945 during a flight from Burg in the 15th prototype, an Ar 234B fitted with two BMW 003s for development trials. He had just taken off, when:

'I noticed a sudden increase in engine noise and an apparent surge in power. I noticed to my amazement that the tachometer of my No 1 engine indicated 11,000 rpm. I instinctively cut the power. This was critical, since I had just taken off and was only about 60 m (200 feet) off the ground. Then I thought about it, and concluded that to have such an excessive engine speed (9,600 rpm was maximum revolutions) the engine would have shed all of its compressor and turbine blades immediately. Therefore the failure had to be in the tachometer itself — the engine could not possibly be turning so fast! And, because the airplane was still 'dirty' — gear and flaps down — I confidently advanced the throttle again to get her around the field. That was my big mistake.'

Suddenly the engine burst into flame, trailing a blazing tail longer than the aircraft itself,

though it is probably fortunate that Kappus, in his enclosed cockpit, never saw it. He pulled the Ar 234B round in a tight circuit and forced it down on the runway; as the aircraft came to a stop a crash truck screeched to a halt beside him and the crew began playing their fire extinguishers on the engine. Once out of the cockpit, Kappus was horrified to see that all of the turbine blades of his port engine had gone, as had the jet nozzle. The flying blades had shot out in all directions, shredding the flap on that side in the process: he afterwards pulled one of the blades out of the self-sealing rubber jacket of the rear fuselage fuel tank.

In fact, the tachometer had been reading correctly the whole time! The fault was tracked down to the shaft to the fuel governor, which had sheared on take-off. The governor, sensing that the engine revolutions had fallen, poured in more and more fuel to the combustion chambers and the engine revolutions ran away out of all control. Kappus had indeed had a lucky escape — had his flight lasted only a few more seconds, the fire would have cut through the aircraft's flying controls and then nothing could have saved him.

During the final weeks of the war 14 Ar 234Cs were built. Diether Lukesch was on the point of forming an operational *Staffel* to test this version in action, when the end came.

When production of the Ar 234 finally ceased in March 1945, with the destruction of the works on the approach of Soviet forces, a total of 210 of these aircraft had been built. In the bomber role this revolutionary new aircraft had been able to achieve little, apart from impressing the enemy with its invulnerability. The 4½ tons of bombs, carried by nine Ar 234s on the largest of the operations by this type, was too small to cause the enemy anything more than a minor inconvenience: Allied bomber forces carried more than ten times this load, even against targets of relatively minor significance. Nor was the Ar 234 able to achieve much as a makeshift night fighter. In its original reconnaissance role, however, the Ar 234 was consistently successful in photographing enemy installations and returning with the precious pictures, usually undetected by the enemy. The irony of the situation was that by the time Germany possessed this capability, her armed forces no longer had the strength to exploit it.

esserschmitt 163

Of the aircraft which went into action during the Second World War the Messerschmitt Me 163 was, without doubt, the least conventional. Not only was it the sole manned rocket-powered aircraft to go into service, but it was also the only tailless design to reach the operational units. Like the Me 262 it started life as a high speed test vehicle for its novel power unit, was then ordered as a fighter and went into action in the summer of 1944. At the end of the conflict the Me 163 was the fastest fighter in service anywhere in the world. Yet its effect on the conflict was minimal. Rarely were more than eight Me163 sorties flown on any one day, and during its entire operational career it shot down probably no more than 16 enemy aircraft.

The Messerschmitt Me 163 stemmed from Alexander Lippisch's DFS 194 flying wing rocket test aircraft, which had first flown during the summer of 1940. As a result of the success of this aircraft, which had reached a maximum speed of 547 kph (341 mph) on the 400 kg (882 pounds) thrust from a Walter liquid fuel rocket motor, Lippisch received an order from the German Air Ministry to design and build three prototypes of an airframe to take Walter's projected new 750 kg (1,650 pound) thrust unit. The new aircraft was designated the Messerschmitt Me 163.

As in the case of the other early German jet aircraft, the airframe of the Me 163 was ready long before the power unit. So the first prototype was flown initially as a glider by test pilot Heini Dittmar, towed off from the airfield at Lechfeld by a Messerschmitt Bf 110 fighter. Like its predecessor, the new aircraft was an unconventional flying-wing design which took off from a jettisonable dolly and landed on a sprung skid. Even by the standards of the day its dimensions were minute: the wingspan was only 9.3 m (30 ft 7 in) and the length was 5.6 m (18 ft 4 in); the leading edge of the wing was swept back at 27 degrees at the root, increasing to 32 degrees for the outboard sections. In the air Dittmar found that the all-wing aircraft handled well. There were some control flutter problems at the higher speeds, but these were soon cured by altering the mass balancing of the surfaces. Once this had been done he was able to reach speeds of over 840 kph (525 mph) during unpowered dives.

In August 1941 the new Walter R II-203

rocket motor was pronounced ready for flight, and installed in the Me 163. On the 13th Dittmar made the first powered flight in the aircraft from Peenemuende West airfield. The Me 163 demonstrated an exceptional turn of speed and, during one of the early tests, Dittmar easily exceeded the current world air speed of 750 kph (469 mph).

The Walter R II-203 ran on two fuels: highly concentrated hydrogen peroxide (*T-Stoff*) and an aqueous solution of sodium or calcium permanganate (*Z-Stoff*). The latter was a benign liquid, but the same cannot be said for the former. Highly concentrated hydrogen peroxide is an unstable compound, liable to decompose on contact with copper, lead or organic material of any sort; and when it decomposes it gives out heat at about the same rate as burning gunpowder. It is highly corrosive, and not its least unendearing feature is that it will burn away human flesh if the liquid is in contact with it for more than a few seconds. The use of this fuel was to pose many problems when the Me 163 later entered service.

Soon after the maiden flight of the Me 163, Rudolf Opitz joined Dittmar in the test programme. Opitz later recounted his first flight in the Me 163 to one of the authors. Following a thorough briefing by Dittmar, Opitz switched on the motor, opened the throttle and started to accelerate across the grass at Peenemuende West. From the beginning, however, Opitz found that his thoughts were 'behind' the rapidly moving rocket aircraft. As

Heini Dittmar preparing to take the DFS 194 experimental rocket aircraft, the predecessor of the Me 163, for a flight on 3 June 1940. *Opposite:* As the rocket aircraft is being pushed to the take-off point, Dittmar follows carrying his flying suit. *Below, left:* Helgo Jahnke makes a final check of the rocket motor, then (above) helps Dittmar into his flying suit. *Bottom, right:* One wing supported by a ground crewman, the rocket motor is started and the diminutive aircraft begins its take-off run. *Willi Elias*

The prototype Me 163A being prepared for its maiden
flight from Peenemuende on 13 August 1941. During
the initial flights the take-off dolly was attached to the
retracted landing ski with no shock absorber or brakes,
which made take-off difficult. *Willi Elias*

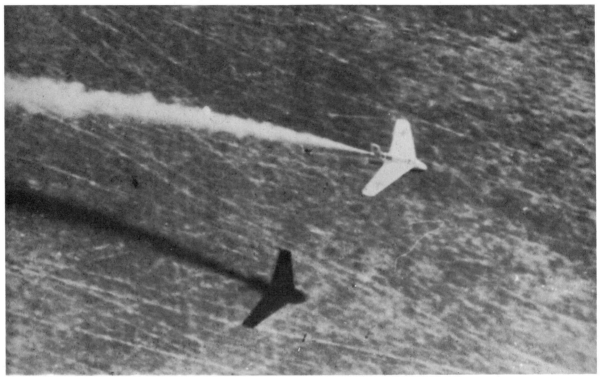

One of the early prototypes making a low altitude powered run over Peenemuende.

a result the machine was about 30 m (100 feet) above the ground before he suddenly realised that the take-off dolly was still attached. Already he was well above the altitude to jettison it safely: if he let it go now the hand-built dolly would almost certainly be wrecked when it smashed into the ground. Not thinking too much about it, Opitz left the dolly in place under the fuselage. He burned off the rest of his fuel, then made a gliding approach and a perfectly normal landing. As he came to a halt, however, excited spectators came running towards him. On the dolly the Me 163 had very little directional control, and they had feared that when the wheels touched the ground the aircraft would have swung violently out of control. Others who later attempted to land the aircraft on its dolly would not be so lucky as Opitz had been.

During the initial flight trials of the Me 163, it became clear that the aircraft was capable of horizontal speeds somewhat greater than those being achieved: during each attempt to get it to its maximum speed, the fuel ran out while the aircraft was still accelerating. To overcome this problem, it was decided to use a Messerschmitt Bf 110 to tow the rocket aircraft to altitude; freed of the need to expend fuel in the take-off and climb, the Me 163 could use all of its fuel for the speed run. Exactly what the maximum speed would be, Lippisch and his design team could only speculate; but the magic figure of 1,000 kph (621 mph) seemed to be within the grasp of the small aircraft.

The great day came on 2 October 1941, when Opitz in the Messerschmitt Bf 110 towed Dittmar in the third prototype off from Peenemuende West for the speed run. The Me 163's fuel tanks were only three-quarters full, but that was to be sufficient. Dittmar cast off the tow at 4,000 m (13,000 feet), started the rocket motor and accelerated rapidly. He took the aircraft to over 975 kph (609 mph) then, without warning, the nose suddenly pitched down violently and he lost control: the Me 163 had gone over its threshold of compressibility. As this happened the rocket motor cut out, the severe negative 'G' forces preventing the fuels from reaching the combustion chamber. The speed rapidly dropped and Dittmar was able to regain control and take the aircraft in for a normal landing.

Post flight examination of the instrumentation carried by the aircraft revealed that immediately before the rocket cut out Dittmar had in fact reached 1,003 kph (just over

Rudolf Opitz joined the Me 163 test programme soon after it began, and later became chief test pilot for the project. *Opitz*

623 mph, or approximately Mach .84 at that altitude). It was a brilliant feat, exceeding the current world air speed record by more than 250 kph (156 mph); and it was probably to remain the fastest manned flight until 1947, when the official world air speed record finally overtook that figure. The dictates of wartime secrecy forbade publication of the Me 163's remarkable flight, however. All that could be done by way of public recognition was the presentation of the Lilienthal Diploma, one of Germany's highest aeronautical awards, to Dittmar, Lippisch and Walter.

The dramatic success of the speed trial aroused considerable enthusiasm from *Generaloberst* Ernst Udet, in charge of Luftwaffe equipment. Less than three weeks after Dittmar's epic flight he approved a plan submitted by Messerschmitt, for the development and construction of 70 Me 163s modified as interceptor fighters. Under the plan the Luftwaffe was to receive sufficient rocket fighters to have a *Gruppe* operational with the type in the spring of 1943. Lippisch immediately began work to redesign the aircraft for the new role, carrying two 20 mm cannon, increased fuel tankage, armour protection for the pilot and full operational equipment. It was planned to power the fighter version with the Walter R II-211 motor, under development with a target thrust of over 1,500 kg (3,300 pounds). The new motor ran on hydrogen peroxide like its predecessor, and a mixture of methyl alcohol, hydrazine hydrate and water (*C-Stoff*).

In the event the development of the fighter version of the Me 163 did not get very far before the death of its most powerful sponsor. In November 1941, less than a month after he had given his approval to the rocket fighter project, Ernst Udet committed suicide. Udet's term of office, in charge of the procurement of aircraft for the Luftwaffe, had been characterised by the fragmentation of the available development effort between numerous projects which were, in several cases, too innovative to be ready for service in the near future. And in the meantime the generation of combat aircraft that should have been entering service, to replace those in use since the beginning of the war — the Me 209, Me 210 and Heinkel He 177 — had all run into difficulties and were far from ready for production. The delays suffered by these projects, and the failure to meet production targets for the types already in service, caused the depression which had culminated in Udet's suicide. *Generalfeldmarschall* Erhard Milch, whose office took over Udet's responsibilities after his death, brought an air of reality to the aircraft production scene. He immediately made sweeping changes aimed at improving the production of current service types, and concentrated the development effort on those new aircraft likely to become operational in the short and the medium term. Long term projects, and those of limited operational use in the current operational stance of the Luftwaffe (and that included the Me 163 fighter), were relegated to positions well down the priority ladder or cancelled altogether. Even with increased tankage the fighter version of Me 163 would carry sufficient fuel for only four minutes' running of the rocket motor, then it would have to glide back to its base. In service, therefore, its role was limited to that of a daylight defence fighter with a radius of action of about 40 km. At the end of 1941, when the German advance into the Soviet Union was halted in front of Moscow and the sole threat to the homeland was from the ineffectual night bombers of the Royal Air Force, the Me 163 offered solutions to none of the Luftwaffe's actual or foreseen problems. Work on the rocket fighter was allowed to continue, but at a low priority.

In the spring of 1942 *Hauptmann* Wolfgang Spaete was appointed Luftwaffe project officer for the Me 163 fighter. And on 26 June the prototype of the fighter version, the Me 163B, made its first unpowered flight from Lechfeld. As usual, the development of the new motor had lagged far behind that of the airframe. Spaete formed a small trials unit, *Erpro-*

Above: On 25 August 1942 the Me 163 was
demonstrated before senior officials and service officers.
Standing in front of the port wing facing left, Opitz
discusses flying the Me 163A with General Adolf
Galland (in leather coat). Left: *Generalfeldmarschall*
Erhard Milch, centre, congratulates Dittmar (in white
flying suit) on an impressive flight. On the extreme right,
wearing a trilby, is Helmuth Walter who designed the
rocket motor. *Willi Elias*

bungskommando 16, to prepare the Me 163B
for service and train pilots to fly it; but initially
the new pilots were able to get rocket experience only on the Me 163A.

Not until June 1943 was the first R II-211
rocket motor, now re-designated the Walter
109-509, delivered to Peenemuende West and
installed in the second prototype Me 163B. On
23rd Rudolf Opitz prepared to take the new
fighter up for its first powered flight. At first
everything went according to plan. The rocket
started normally and, after a quick check that
everything was functioning as it should, Opitz
advanced the throttle through each of its three

stages. With a piercing roar the aircraft accelerated across the grass but, just before it reached
flying speed, the take-off dolly wrenched itself
away from the fuselage. By now Opitz was too
close to the airfield boundary to stop, so he
gritted his teeth and held the throttle open,
continuing to accelerate bumpily on his landing
skid. Finally, to his great relief, the aircraft
lifted off the ground. The German pilot's
troubles were not yet over, however. As he
eased back on the stick to begin his climb, the
cockpit began to fill with stinging hydrogen
peroxide fumes: in wrenching itself free, the
take-off dolly had fractured one of the fuel

lines. Opitz's eyes began to burn and then, even more disconcerting, the glass inside the cockpit and that of his flying goggles became covered with a thickening white film. Just when it seemed he might have to bale out, the motor devoured the last of the fuel; slowly the fumes began to clear, and with them the white film on the glass. Shaken by his two narrow escapes, Opitz returned to the airfield and made a normal landing.

During the weeks that followed several Walter 109-509 motors were delivered, and installed in Me 163Bs. Test-flying these as they became ready, Rudolf Opitz had further adventures. On 30 July, after a rapid climb at full throttle to 8,150 m (26,500 feet), he felt the rocket's thrust begin to fluctuate violently and saw the fire warning light flashing on. Opitz shut down the rocket and the light went out. During the subsequent descent he tried to re-start the rocket but it defied all of his efforts. With a large quantity of unburnt fuel still in the tanks he was in an unenviable position: the Me 163 would land faster than normal, and any accident that caused the tanks to fracture and the fuels to come together would result in a

Above: Heini Dittmar flying one of the early Me 163Bs. *Transit Films*

Top: An Me 163B in front of one of the engine test buildings at Peenemuende. Note the running water hose playing on the concrete behind the aircraft, indicating that the aircraft has either just been refuelled, or is about to be. This was a necessary safety precaution, to dilute any rocket fuel spilled during refuelling. *Transit Films*

Top: Refuelling an Me 163B with *C-Stoff* (mixture of methyl alchohol, hydrazine hydrate and water). When the tanks are full the aircraft will settle on the wooden stabilising posts under the wings, which prevent it rocking while it is being worked on. *Transit Films*

Right: Trailing steam and shock waves, an Me 163B begins its take-off run.

Opposite centre and below: Close-ups of an Me 163B after it has skidded to a halt at the end of its landing run, dropping one wing. *Transit Films*

Top: An Me 163B photographed immediately after take-off, releasing its undercarriage dolly at a height of about 10 m (about 30 ft). *Transit Films*

Above: This early system for recovering the Me 163 after it had landed employed inflated air bags to lift the aircraft; note the compressed air bottles attached to the top of the V-shaped towing arms. *Transit Films*

violent explosion. Opitz's only alternative was
to bale out, but this would have meant the loss
of one of the few available Me 163Bs; he
decided to land the aircraft, and did so successfully.

On the following day Opitz had more
problems. The tests called for accurate measurements of some of the rocket motor's para-
meters, and to allow room for the necessary
additional test instrumentation Opitz agreed to
the removal of the artificial horizon and the
turn-and-bank indicator from his instrument
panel. For this trial Opitz wore a small camera
attached to a band round his head, with which
he could photograph the instruments at regular
intervals. In a letter to one of the authors he
described the flight that followed; it was
memorable, even by Me 163 standards:

'The day for the flight test was cloudless but hazy
and the programme called for take-off to the north-
east, establishing a maximum power climb at
510 kph (320 mph) indicated air speed on a straight
line out over the Baltic, taking pictures of the
instrument panel at 500 m (1,600 feet) intervals up
to an altitude of 12,300 m (40,000 feet). It seemed
to be simple enough. However, the time schedule
for taking the data was not easy to comply with
when one realises that the aircraft needed only ten
seconds to climb to 500 m after reaching the desired
airspeed and only six seconds were needed to climb
through 500 m at higher altitudes.

Take-off, dropping the dolly, retracting the
flaps, accelerating to desired airspeed and trimming
the aircraft for proper climb angle kept me very
busy prior to recording my first checkpoint. The
eight to ten seconds available between each of the
following checkpoints were just enough to scan the
instrument panel and to make necessary control
adjustments to hold the aircraft within the narrow
operating limits specified for the test. For a while
everything went fine and I met the recording points
right on the dot.

My airspeed, however, started to increase during the climb toward the 5,000 m (16,400 feet)
check point and despite corrective action I missed
the required airspeed. I raised my head to look
outside for a quick check of aircraft attitude against
the horizon, only to find that it was not visible
because I was climbing in a heavy haze that blended
perfectly with the sea below.'

Too late, Opitz realised that in trying to do
too many things at once he had become dangerously disorientated; and with two of his
most important flight instruments removed

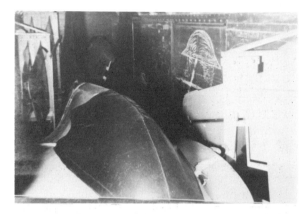

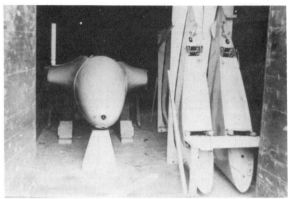

Above: Because of its short range, the Me 163 had to be
transported from the factories to the service airfields by
rail. The photographs show one of these aircraft
dismantled and fitted in a box car. *Willi Elias*

Below: When the two rocket fuels came together they
released energy at the same rate as gunpowder. This is
all that remained of an Me 163B after the two fuels had
come together inadvertently. *Opitz*

from the panel he had no way of discovering what the aircraft was doing. The next thing he knew was that the nose suddenly dropped and the motor cut — a sure sign that he had exceeded the compressibility threshold and was now diving out of control. Desperately he searched outside the cockpit for a reference point, and found a small island disconcertingly high on his canopy: he was in a steep diving turn to the left. Acting instinctively, Opitz was able to pull the Messerschmitt out of its dive just a few hundred metres above the flat-calm sea.

'Heading now for the coastline, which loomed out of the haze in the distance, I restarted the engine successfully and within minutes appeared over the airfield for a safe landing, much to the relief of our anxious crew who had given up hopes for my safe return after observing the aircraft arcing to the left during the steep climb and then suddenly heading down just as steeply toward the sea and disappearing below the horizon from their point of observation.

A walk-around inspection of the Me 163 after the landing quickly revealed signs attesting to the high speeds and stresses to which I had unintentionally subjected the aircraft. The rudder had disintegrated completely; only its spar was still attached to the vertical fin. Fairing fasteners on the fuselage and wings had pulled out of their seatings.'

Gradually pilots and ground crewmen became more familiar with the Me 163B and the trials programme became less of an adventure, though always one had to be careful. The pilots and those on the ground liable to come into contact with the hydrogen peroxide wore special overalls made of a non-organic asbestos-based fibre. Yet although the material did give partial protection against small quantities of

the rocket fuel, if there was a major spillage the liquid was able to soak through the seams of the garment and reach the man inside.

At an all-up weight of the Me 163B on take-off of 3,950 kg (8,700 pounds), just over half or 2,018 kg (4,440 pounds) was fuel for the rocket motor. And this allowed only about four minutes' running at full power, for with the throttle in the fully open position the Walter 109-509 devoured about 8.3 kg (18.3 pounds) of the two chemical fuels *each second*. Once the fuel was gone the greatly lightened Me 163B became a glider, though one with excellent handling characteristics. Rudolf Opitz remembers that the aircraft was light on the controls and the low speed handling was first class; it was, he recounted, 'absolutely spin-proof'.

By August 1943 construction of the pre-production batch of 70 Me 163Bs was progressing well at the Messerschmitt factory at Obertraubling near Regensburg. At the same time the Klemm factory, near Stuttgart, was getting ready to build the aircraft of the main production batch, working under Messerschmitt supervision. Then, on the 17th of that month, the programme suffered a double blow. During the day USAAF heavy bombers hit the Messerschmitt plant at Regensburg, destroying 11 brand-new Me 163Bs and causing serious disruption to Messerschmitt 109 production. And that night Royal Air Force Bomber Command struck at Peenemuende, where Spaete's *Erprobungskommando* was based.

After the attack on Regensburg, and the need to concentrate everything on restoring production of the Messerschmitt 109, responsibility for producing the Me 163 became that of Klemm alone with very little help from the parent company. And Klemm, a small firm which previously had built only light aircraft, was to prove quite unequal to the task of turning out such a high performance combat aircraft in quantity.

Following the attack on Peenemuende *Erprobungskommando 16* moved to the nearby airfield at Anklam, where the training of pilots continued.

The training programme for new pilots began with a few flights in short-spanned gliders, to familiarise trainees with the problems of handling such aircraft. Next came towed flights in Me 163As first with empty tanks, then with

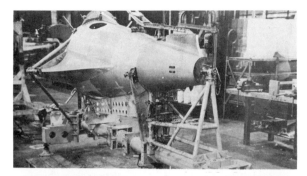

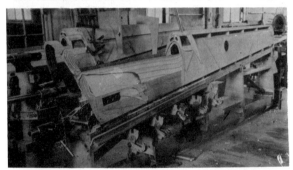

progressively larger amounts of water ballast in the fuel tanks to increase the landing speed. This phase of the training culminated in three powered flights in the Me 163A, with progressively larger amounts of fuel.

Now the pilots were ready to fly the Me 163B, which was somewhat heavier than its predecessor. Starting the Walter 109-509 motor was relatively simple. The throttle had five notched positions: Off, Idle, 1st Stage, 2nd Stage and 3rd Stage. When the throttle was moved from Off to Idle, this exposed the starter button. When the button was pressed, small quantities of the rocket fuels were allowed to run into the auxiliary combustion chamber; on reacting, the two chemicals drove a turbine which pumped the fuels into the main combustion chamber in the ratio of 3.25 parts of hydrogen peroxide to each part of hydrazine hydrate. The thrust of the motor built up rapidly to about 100 kg (220 pounds). After a check of his two engine instruments — a fuel pump tachometer and a main combustion chamber pressure gauge — that the indications were normal, the pilot would advance his throttle through the 1st and 2nd Stages, gradually increasing the thrust. Finally, if all was still in order, he pushed the throttle to the 3rd Stage and the motor ran up to full thrust. The small fighter rode over the tiny chocks under the dolly wheels and began to pick up speed rapidly.

When it reached about 280 kph (175 mph) the fully-laden Me 163B would lift itself off the ground and a couple of seconds later, at about 10 m (30 feet) above the ground, the pilot released the take-off dolly. Freed of the drag,

Left, top to bottom: Me 163 components in production at one of the Klemm factories near Stuttgart; building up the metal fuselage and tail section; construction of the wooden leading edge of the wing. A completed wing, showing the spaces in front of and behind the main spar to house the wing *C-Stoff* tanks.

Opposite: Rudolf Opitz preparing to get airborne in an Me 163B from Bad Zwischenahn. Because of the dangers from inhaling hydrogen peroxide fumes if there was any leakage, and also because of the aircraft's very high rate of climb, the oxygen mask was worn from take off. *Transit Films*

the rocket fighter accelerated still faster. On reaching about 700 kph (435 mph) in horizontal flight, still accelerating, the pilot would ease back on his stick to pull the Me 163 into a zoom climb at an angle of about 45 degrees with hardly any drop in forwards speed. Held in the climb at full throttle, the rocket fighter reached 6,000 m (just under 20,000 feet) in about 2 minutes 16 seconds.

So far so good. But initially the Walter HWK 109-509 motor demonstrated a disconcerting habit of shutting down as the pilot eased forwards on his stick to level out at the top of the climb. And, for technical reasons, the rocket motor could not be re-started for at least two minutes after the shut-down. All in all this was a crippling tactical deficiency, since the shut-down occurred just at the time when, during a real operational mission, the Me 163 pilot would be in contact with the enemy and about to begin his attack. The task of tracking down the cause of the problem was to exercise Walter engineers for some months, for it proved impossible to reproduce the top-of-climb 'G' forces during bench running tests on the ground.

Considering the dangers inherent in the rocket fighter programme, it is remarkable that it continued as long as it did without a fatal flying accident. The first to lose his life in this way was a trainee pilot *Oberfeldwebel* Alois Woerndl, who took off under power in an Me 163A on 30 November. Gliding back with empty fuel tanks, he misjudged his approach and was killed when his aircraft flipped over on to its back after a very heavy landing. As is so often the case in flying accidents, this one had nothing to do with the really hazardous aspects of operating the aircraft.

Exactly a month later, on 30 December, *Oberleutnant* Joachim Poehs lost his life also while flying an Me 163A. Just after lift-off he released his dolly too soon; it rebounded off the airfield and struck the fuselage, causing the rocket motor to cut out. Banking his aircraft to land back on the field, Poehs hit a flak emplacement and the Me 163 smashed into the ground.

The opening of 1944 brought with it a severe deterioration of the military situation in the skies over Germany, for the Luftwaffe air defence units charged with countering the American daylight raids; now the latest versions of the P-47 and P-51 escort fighters were

proving able to penetrate deeper and deeper into the Reich to cover the attacks. At last there was a clear requirement for a high performance target defence fighter such as the Me 163, even if it did have only a limited endurance. The armament of two 20 mm cannon was too light to be effective against the tough American heavy bombers, so new Me 163Bs were to be fitted with a pair of 30 mm MK 108 cannon.

Suddenly the Me 163 was back in favour again, and in an effort to speed it into operational service the Luftwaffe High Command issued orders in January for the formation of 20th *Staffel* of *Jagdgeschwader* 1, to be based at Bad Zwischenahn near Oldenburg with a strength of 12 Me 163s. The following month, under the command of *Oberleutnant* Robert Olejnik but still far short of its complement of both aircraft and trained pilots, the unit was re-designated 1st *Staffel* of *Jagdgeschwader* 400. With one of the first operationally equipped Me 163s to be delivered, Rudolf Opitz flew a series of interceptions against simulated enemy bomber formations at altitudes between 6,000 and 8,000 m (20,000 and 26,000 feet). But during each of them the motor cut when he levelled out the aircraft at the top of the climb; the old problem remained with the rocket fighter. Early in March the *Staffel* moved to Wittmundhafen, now with five aircraft and a dozen pilots in various stages of training.

In spite of all efforts to get the Me 163 into action as soon as possible, deliveries of new aircraft from the Klemm company remained painfully slow. Not until 13 May was Wolfgang Spaete, recently promoted to Major, ready to attempt the first operational interception in a rocket fighter. After taking off from Bad Zwischenahn, Spaete was vectored on to a pair of P-47s flying near the airfield. Just as he was about to close in for the attack, however, his rocket motor cut out and he was forced to break away; fortunately for the German pilot, he had not been seen. Spaete now spent a frustrating couple of minutes before he could re-start the motor, watching his quarry getting smaller and smaller as they left him far behind. Finally the wait was up and, re-starting the rocket, he accelerated after them. Spaete overhauled the enemy fighters rapidly and swung into a firing position. Then suddenly, as he had one of the P-47s in his sight and was about to open fire, his left wing dropped violently: in

concentrating on his prey, Spaete had allowed his speed to build up too far and the Me 163 had exceeded its compressibility threshold. By the time he regained control of the plunging rocket fighter, there was insufficient fuel left for a further interception. Blissfully unaware of their narrow escape, the American fighters pilots continued on their heading. Doubly frustrated, Spaete burned off the remainder of his fuel and returned to his base.

Further attempts to intercept Allied aircraft during the days that followed proved similarly unsuccessful. But on 31 May a reconnaissance Spitfire of the Royal Air Force brought back the first reliable report of a sighting of an Me 163 in the air, near Wilhelmshaven. The official report on the incident stated:

'Flying at 37,000 feet the pilot first saw a white trail about 3,000 feet below him and something over a mile distant horizontally. The trail turned into an interception course and then disappeared. The Spitfire pilot began a climb, and during the next three minutes saw the trail reappear four times, at intervals, as the unknown aircraft climbed towards him. He observed that the plane apparently covered a distance of about three times the length of the visible trail before the next emission would appear.

By the time the Spitfire had reached 41,000 feet the pilot could see the supposed enemy, but could not identify the aircraft, except that it seemed to be "nearly all wing" which possibly had a marked sweep-back. At this point the unknown aircraft was only 3,000 feet below the Spitfire, and only about 1,000 yards away horizontally. Evidently it had climbed about 8,000 feet and reduced the horizontal distance by about 1,000 yards during the time it took the Spitfire to climb about 3,500 feet. No further trails were seen, the pilot lost sight of the aircraft and soon afterwards returned to base.

The reported regularity of the appearance of vapour trails tends to bear out previous reports that the propulsion unit of the Me 163 is used only intermittently, and also suggests that it is cut in and out automatically. On the other hand this apparent regularity may have been mere coincidence.'[1]

The report concluded with the observation that the Me 163 may have been on a training flight, since the incident occurred only some 20 miles from Bad Zwischenahn where these aircraft had been photographed on the ground.

---

[1]When the Me 163 pilot throttled back to less than full thrust the visible smoke trail ceased; the rocket motor had not cut out.

Top: Me 163B of *Erprobungskommando 16* beginning a rocket take-off from Bad Zwischenahn. *Transit Films*

Above: Steam gushes from the fuel pump turbine exhaust, as the ground crewman pushes the electrical trolley clear prior to starting the rocket motor.

Above, right: *Oberst* Gordon Gollob, the famous fighter ace, who took over from Wolfgang Spaete as leader of the Me 163 fighter project in June 1944. *Gollob*

Two Me 163s (circled) of the five belonging to *Erprobungskommando 16* **which were photographed at Bad Zwischenahn by an Allied reconnaissance aircraft on 11 May 1944.** *USAF*

By now the main cause of the Me 163's motor cutting out at the top of the climb had been discovered. The two chemical fuels had to be injected into the combustion chamber in exactly the right ratio, or an uncontrolled explosion might result. As a safety measure, the Walter rocket was designed to shut itself down *automatically* if there was a break in the supply of either of the fuels. When the Me 163 was levelled out at the top of the climb, however, the change of attitude of the aircraft caused the fuels to slop about in their tanks; if a feed pipe was momentarily uncovered the safety system would detect a break in the fuel supply, and shut down the motor. The installation of additional baffle plates in the fuel tanks reduced the incidence of cut-outs, but did not prevent them altogether.

In June 1944, still without a successful engagement to its credit, the Me 163 *Staffel* was redesignated Ist *Gruppe* of JG 400, re-

ceived a new commander, and was redeployed. On his promotion *Major* Wolfgang Spaete was sent to command a conventional fighter *Gruppe* on the Eastern Front; in his place as Me 163 project leader was appointed the fighter ace and leader *Oberst* Gordon Gollob. Spaete's plan for the deployment of the rocket fighter had called for a series of specially equipped airfields at approximately 100 km (62 mile) intervals — ie all within Me 163 gliding range — positioned in an arc through northern Germany and Holland astride the American bombers' routes to their targets. But by the early part of June this plan had been overtaken by events.

Once the Allied troops had established their bridgehead in Normandy, the US Strategic Bomber commander General Carl Spaatz ordered that henceforth the *primary strategic aim* of the 8th Air Force in England and the 15th Air Force in Italy was to be the destruction of the enemy fuel supplies. The effect of the resultant massed air attacks on the German synthetic oil refineries was immediate and devastating: from 175,000 tons in April, the German production of high octane aviation petrol fell to less than a third of that figure — only 55,000 tons — in June.

The few available Me 163s at bases in northern Germany could easily be avoided by the American bombers coming in from England; and they were no threat at all to the bombers coming in from Italy. So Gollob now ordered I./JG 400 to concentrate its aircraft at the airfield at Brandis near Leipzig in southeastern Germany. The Me 163 was to be used as a target-defence fighter, to protect the vitally important oil refineries at Leuna-Merseburg, Bohlen, Zeitz and Luetzkendorf, all of which were coming under repeated attack.

The move to Brandis took about three weeks to complete, and not until the latter part of July was JG 400 ready to make any serious attempt to engage enemy aircraft. Then, on the morning of the 29th, a force of 596 American bombers set out to attack the Leuna-Merseberg complex. As the raiders began their bombing runs, six Me 163Bs scrambled off the ground at Brandis in succession and climbed steeply to intercept. Colonel Avelin Tacon, leading P-51s of the 359th Fighter Group escorting the bombers in the target area, afterwards reported:

'I encountered two Me 163s. My eight P-51s were furnishing close escort for a combat wing of B-17s, and we were flying south at 25,000 feet when one of my pilots called in two contrails at six o'clock high some five miles back at 32,000 feet. I identified them immediately as jet propelled aircraft. Their contrails could not be mistaken and looked very dense and white, somewhat like an elongated cumulus cloud some three quarters of a mile in length. My section turned 180 degrees back toward the enemy fighters, which included two with jets turned on and three in a glide without jets operating at the moment.

The two I had spotted made a diving turn to the left in close formation and feinted towards the bombers at six o'clock, cutting off their jets as they turned. Our flight turned for a head-on pass to get between them and the rear of the bomber formation. While still 3,000 yards from the bombers, they turned into us and left the bombers alone. In this turn they banked about 80 degrees but their course changed only about 20 degrees. Their turn radius was very large but their rate of roll appeared

excellent. Their speed I estimated was 500 to 600 miles per hour. Both planes passed under us, 1,000 feet below, while still in a close formation glide. In an attempt to follow them, I split S'd. One continued down in a 45 degree dive, the other climbed up into the sun very steeply and I lost him. Then I looked back at the one in a dive and saw he was five miles away at 10,000 feet. Other members of my flight reported that the one which went up into the sun used his jet in short bursts as though it was blowing smoke rings. These pilots appeared very experienced but not aggressive.'

Tacon's final comment was a perceptive one, for some of the German pilots had trouble with their motors cutting out at the top of the climb — it was difficult to be aggressive if this happened. Those Me 163 pilots who were able to reach the bombers found that their closing speeds were so great that none was able to score hits. Harried by the escorting Mustangs, the rocket fighters exhausted their fuel and returned to Brandis. But there another problem awaited them. Gliding down one after the other, the Me 163s were committed to landing; and they did so in rapid succession, giving the ground crewmen no time to clear the rocket fighters from the landing ground. Fortunately for the German pilots there were no collisions between landing aircraft and those already down, but there were some near misses. It was a clear pointer to the problems that would arise in the future if several Me 163s were to operate simultaneously from one airfield.

After reading Tacon's report Major General William Kepner, commanding the 8th Fighter Command, instructed his operational units:

'... It is believed we can expect to see more of these aircraft immediately and we can expect attacks on the bombers from the rear in formations or waves. To be able to counter and have time to turn into them, our units are going to have to be in positions relatively close to the bombers to be between them and our heavies. It is believed these tactics will keep them from making effective, repeat effective, attacks on the bombers ...'

The fear of a massed attack by the rocket fighters was to remain with the US High Command for the remainder of the war though, for the reasons already outlined, such a move would have presented considerable tactical difficulties for I./JG 400. Kepner's order for the US escort fighters to stay closer to the bombers

Me 163

 1 Generator drive propeller
 2 Generator
 3 Compressed air bottle
 4 Battery and electronics packs
 5 Cockpit ventilation intake
 6 Solid armour (15 mm) nose cone
 7 Accumulator pressuriser
 8 Direct cockpit air intake
 9 FuG 16 radio panel
10 Rudder control assembly
11 Hydraulic and compressed air points
12 Elevon control rocker-bar
13 Control relay
14 Flying controls assembly box

15 Plastic rudder pedals
16 Radio tuning controls
17 Torque shaft
18 Port T-stoff cockpit tank (13 Imp gal/60 l capacity)
19 Control column
20 Hinged instrument panel
21 Laminated glass windscreen brace
22 Revi 16B gunsight
23 Laminated glass internal windscreen (90 mm)
24 Armament and radio switches (starboard console)
25 Pilot's seat
26 Back armour (8 mm)
27 Head and shoulder armour (13 mm)
28 Radio frequency selector pack

29 Headrest
30 Mechanically-jettisonable hinged canopy
31 Ventilation panel
32 Fixed leading-edge wing slot
33 Trim tab
34 Fabric-covered starboard elevon
35 Position of underwing landing flap
36 Inboard trim flap
37 FuG 16 receiving aerial
38 T-Stoff filler cap

39 Main unprotected T-Stoff fuselage tank (229 Imp gal/1,040 l capacity)
40 Aft cockpit glazing
41 Port cannon ammunition box (60 rounds)
42 Starboard cannon ammunition box (60 rounds)
43 Ammunition feed chute
44 T-Stoff starter tank
45 Rudder control upper bell crank
46 C-Stoff filler cap
47 HWK 509A-1 motor turbine housing
48 Main rocket motor mounting frame
49 Rudder control rod
50 Disconnect point
51 Aerial matching unit
52 Fin front spar/fuselage attachment point
53 Tailfin construction
54 Rudder horn balance
55 Rudder upper hinge
56 Rudder frame

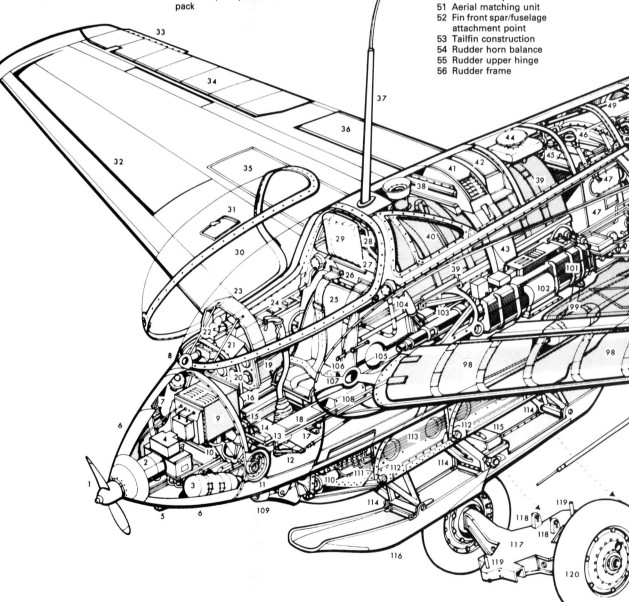

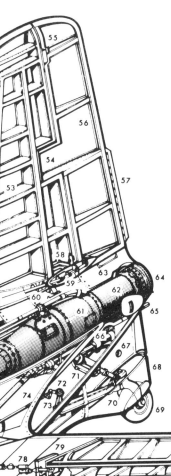

57	Rudder trim tab
58	Rudder control rocker-bar
59	Linkage fairing
60	Fin rear spar/fuselage attachment point
61	Rocket motor combustion chamber
62	Tailpipe
63	Rudder root fairing
64	Rocket thrust orifice
65	Vent pipe outlet
66	Hydraulic cylinder
67	Lifting point
68	Tailwheel fairing
69	Steerable tailwheel
70	Tailwheel axle fork
71	Tailwheel oleo
72	Tailwheel steering linkage
73	Coupling piece/vertical lever
74	Wingroot fillet
75	Combustion chamber support brace
76	Gun-cocking mechanism
77	Trim flap control angle gear (bulkhead mounted)
78	Worm gear
79	Trim flap mounting
80	Port inboard trim flap
81	Elevon mounting
82	Rocker-bar
83	Elevon actuation push-rod
84	Port elevon
85	Wing rear spar
86	Trim tab

87	Elevon outboard hinge
88	Wingtip bumper
89	Wing construction
90	Fixed leading-edge wing slot
91	Elevon control bell crank
92	Position of port underwing landing flap
93	Push-rod in front spar
94	Front spar
95	FuG 25a aerial
96	Pitot head
97	Wing tank connecting-pipe fairing
98	C-Stoff leading-edge tank (16 Imp gal/73 l capacity)
99	Gun-cocking compressed air bottle
100	Main C-Stoff wing tank (36 Imp gal/173 l capacity)
101	Port 30 mm MK 108 short-barrel cannon
102	Spent cartridge and link chute
103	Gun forward mounting frame
104	Pressure-tight gun-control passage
105	Blast tube
106	Gun alignment mechanism
107	Cannon port
108	FuG 25a IFF pack

109	Tow-bar attachment point
110	Compressed-air ram for landing skid
111	Hydraulics and compressed-air pipes
112	Landing skid pivots
113	Landing skid keel mounting
114	Landing skid mounting brackets
115	Trolley jettison mechanism
116	Landing skid
117	Take-off trolley frame
118	Take-off trolley retaining lugs
119	Take-off trolley alignment pins
120	Low-pressure tyre

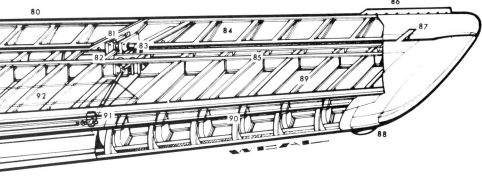

MESSERSCHMITT 163B

Power unit: one Walter HWK 509 rocket motor, rated at 1,700 kg (3,750 pounds) thrust.

Armament: early versions carried two 20 mm Mauser MG 151 cannon. Later versions carried two 30 mm Rheinmetall Borsig MK 108 cannon with 60 rounds per gun.

Performance: maximum speed 955 kph (592 mph) above 3,000 m (9,750 ft). Approximate operational radius of action 40 km (25 miles). Initial climb 81 m/sec (15,900 feet per minute). Time to 6,000 m (19,500 ft), 2 min 16 secs.

Weights: Empty, equipped, 1,908 kg (4,205 pounds); normally loaded, 4,310 kg (9,500 pounds).

Dimensions: Span 9.33 m (30 ft 7½ in) Length 5.85 m (19 ft 2½ in) Wing area 18.5 sq m (199 sq ft).

Above: The instrument panel of the Me 163B, showing the relatively sparce instrumentation required for the rocket fighter. The tanks on either side of the pilot's legs contained *T-Stoff* (highly concentrated hydrogen peroxide). *Crown Copyright*

Right: Towing an Me 163B on its dolly, using the *Scheuschlepper* lightweight three-wheeled tug.

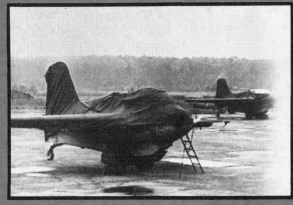

Opposite and left: Me 163Bs of Ist *Gruppe* of Jagdgeschwader 400 at readiness at Brandis.

was a sound one: by maintaining a continual threat on the Me 163s while they were in the vicinity of the bombers, the German pilots would be forced to keep their speed high as they made their attacking runs — with a consequent reduction in the accuracy of their shooting.

On the following day, the 29th, a force of 647 US heavy bombers attacked Merseburg. This time six Me 163s attempted to intercept the raiders but, as on the first day, the results were inconclusive and neither side suffered damage.

On 31 July a reconnaissance Lightning had a brush with an Me 163 but succeeded in escaping without damage. And on 5 August no fewer than ten rocket fighters were reported in the vicinity of another American bomber formation attacking Merseburg, though yet again there appears to have been no loss on either side.

Not until 16 August was there a real fight between Ist *Gruppe* of *Jagdgeschwader* 400 and a US raiding force. On that day 1,096 B-17s and B-24s, with a powerful fighter escort, set out to attack targets at Zeitz, Rositz, Leuna, Boehlen, Halle, Dresden and Koethen. Five Me 163Bs were waiting at readiness and these scrambled into the air. One of the first to reach the bombers was *Feldwebel* Herbert Straznicky, who dived to attack a B-17 of the 305th Bomb Group. Sergeant H. Kaysen, the bomber's tail gunner, kept up an accurate fire on the rocket fighter as it ran in and when the latter broke away at short range it was streaming black smoke. Suffering from splinter wounds to his left arm and thigh, Straznicky was forced to bale out of his crippled aircraft. He reached the ground without further injury.

Shortly afterwards *Leutnant* Hartmut Ryll attacked another of the 305th BG B-17s, that piloted by 2nd Lieutenant C. Laverdiere. Closing in to short range, Ryll's accurate burst scored hits on both inboard engines and the flaps and killed one of the waist gunners and the ball gunner.

Pulling away from the bomber formation, Ryll then spotted B-17 'Outhouse Mouse' of the 91st Bomb Group straggling behind the main force of bombers after having suffered damage during an attack by FW 190s. As the Me 163 closed in for the coup de grâce, however, it was in its turn spotted by Lieutenant Colonel John Murphy leading a pair of P-51s of the 359th Fighter Group. Murphy afterwards reported:

'I was escorting our bombers south-east of Leipzig at 27,000 ft when I noticed a contrail climbing rapidly up toward the bombers from behind and the port side. I recognized the contrails as being produced by a jet-propelled aircraft because of its speed. Due to its speed and altitude advantage I knew I could not overtake him, but noticed a straggling B-17 to the starboard at 25,000 ft which was headed north-east of Leipzig all alone, and I headed toward him, thinking that he probably would be attacked. The Jettie contrail ceased about 500 yds from the bomber, and from that point on I kept him in sight as I would any other aircraft. He passed through the bombers and down to the straggling B-17 and arrived there before I could; however, I wasn't far behind and was overtaking. After he passed the B-17 he seemed to level off, and as I closed on him I opened fire from about 1,000 ft and held it until I overshot. I scored a few hits on the left side of the fuselage. I pulled up to the left as sharply as I could to prevent overshooting and getting out in front of him and lost sight of both him and my wingman. My wingman, Lt Jones, reported that the Jettie flipped over on his back in a half roll, and as he did so, he scored a sufficient number of hits on the canopy to destroy him. As Jones tried to follow him through on his dive, Jones blacked out. When I completed my sharp chandelle turn to the left, I saw another Jettie off to my left and Jones farther off and lower to my right. I started down on this one, which was making rather shallow diving turns to the left. I think I must have turned with him through two turns before overtaking him. I realized that I was going to overtake him rapidly too, but I held my fire to an estimated 750 ft and held a continuous burst, seeing continuous strikes the full length of his fuselage. Parts began falling off, followed by a big explosion and more parts falling off. I could smell the strange chemical fumes in my cockpit as I followed through the smoke of the explosion. It seemed to me that a large chunk of the fuselage from the canopy on back just popped off with the explosion.'

Top: Me 163B of Jagdgeschwader 400 commencing a rocket take-off from Brandis. *Glogner*

Above: Retrieval of an Me 163B after landing, using the system employed late in the war. Again the *Scheuschlepper* vehicle was used, this time with a tracked trailer with two hydraulic arms which lifted the aircraft clear off the ground.

Murphy followed the falling aircraft some way down then, seeing another enemy aircraft about two miles off, broke off the chase. By now his P-51 was running low on fuel so he turned for home. At the end of his report he stated:

'My first impression when I saw the jet plane was that I was standing still. It seemed hopeless to try to attempt to overtake them, but my actions were prompted by a curiosity to get as close to them as possible. I believe that will be the reaction of every pilot that comes in contact with them. Another thing that is very noticeable is that their speed varies considerably, but it's hard to realize this until you find yourself rapidly overtaking them.'

From the German evidence available, it seems clear that the first Me 163 to be destroyed by Murphy and Jones was Ryll's; he was killed. The second Me 163 may possibly have been Straznicky's after he had baled out; it is known that this aircraft exploded before it struck the ground. Without having yet scored a kill, the rocket fighter unit had lost its first two aircraft in combat.

Eight days later, on 24 August, I./JG 400 scored its first successes. Eight Me 163Bs were launched from Brandis to engage a large force of B-17s approaching Leuna, and shortly afterwards crewmen of the 92nd, 305th, 381st and 457th Bomb Groups were reporting the approach of the small rocket fighters. Badly positioned by their ground controller, *Feldwebel* Siegfried Schubert and his wingman climbed to about 10,000 m (32,500 feet) without sighting the bombers. Both Me 163s throttled back to idling to conserve fuel and descended in the glide, searching for their prey.

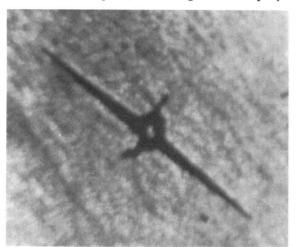

Above: The B-17 flown by 2nd Lieutenant C. Laverdiere of the 305th Bomb Group, after being shot up by *Leutnant* Hartmut Ryll on 16 August 1944. Left: Ryll's Me 163 photographed shortly afterwards during its final moments, under fire from the P-51 flown by Lieutenant Colonel John Murphy of the 359th Fighter Group; the German pilot was killed during the action. *USAF*

Opposite right: Two of the rocket pilots of JG 400 who fought during the August actions: *Feldwebeln* Manfred Eisenmann (left) and Rudolf Glogner. Eisenmann was killed when his Me 163 crashed on 24 August. *Glogner*

Far right: *Feldwebel* Rudolf Zimmermann with 'Harras', the mascot of 1st *Staffel* of Jagdgeschwader 400. *Zimmermann*

They were below the level of the bombers when the two German pilots finally sighted their prey: the B-17s of the 92nd Bomb Group. Both Me 163s immediately opened up to full power and swung round into the attack. Schubert singled out the leading B-17 piloted by Lieutenant Hoehler, and his short burst caused severe damage to the left wing; the bomber staggered out of the formation losing height, to crash shortly afterwards. Still with his rocket motor full on Schubert ran rapidly underneath his victim and clear of the bombers' return fire; but in his haste to get away he ran into compressibility trouble and suddenly found himself diving out of control. While Schubert wrestled with his stick his wingman made a similarly accurate firing pass on 2nd Lieutenant Steve Nagy's B-17; its No. 4 engine burst into flame, the aircraft went into a spin and it blew up at about 5,800 m (19,000 feet).

Two other Me 163s piloted by *Oberfeldwebel* Peter Husser and *Unteroffizier* Manfred Eisenmann then darted in to attack the same bomber formation; no American bombers were hit during their firing runs, however, though Eisenmann's Messerschmitt suffered tail damage from the return fire.

By now Schubert had regained control of his plunging aircraft and, having restarted his motor, accelerated back to altitude to regain the fray. This time he made contact with B-17s of the 457th Bomb Group and, throttling back to idling, attacked from almost head-on in a shallow dive. Schubert's rounds scored hits on Lieutenant Winfred Pugh's B-17, which peeled away from the formation and went into a spin, before finally blowing up at about 3,000 m (10,000 ft).

Also at about the same time, B-17s of the 305th Bomb Group came under attack from a pair of Me 163s and one of the bombers, piloted by 2nd Lieutenant P. Dabney, was shot down. In each case the rocket fighter pilots were able to carry out their attacking runs so rapidly that they were clear of the bombers before the escorting Mustangs could intervene.

Still there were technical problems with the Me 163, however; it seemed that as some of the problems were solved, new ones arose to replace them. Climbing out to intercept *Feldwebel* Rudolf Zimmermann had his rocket motor prematurely cut out. Unable to restart it he pulled the handle to jettison the dangerous hydrogen peroxide, then turned through a semi-circle and headed back to Brandis.[1] Lacking the necessary altitude for a normal approach, he extended his skid and lined up for a straight-in approach and a down-wind landing. He later wrote:

'Coming in fast and short, I touched down early and hard. At that moment there was a tremendous explosion with flames, smoke and fragments of the aircraft flying round the cockpit. When the machine came to a halt I could see the grass landing ground through a hole in the bottom of the cockpit. Around the skid all the metal skinning had been blown away and the plywood covering on the underside of the wings had also been torn open.'

Zimmermann received a severe reprimand from his *Staffel* commander, for supposedly causing the damage by landing the Me 163 too hard. Only somewhat later, after a similar but more serious incident in which an aircraft was wrecked and its pilot badly burned, was the true cause of the explosion discovered. After being jettisoned, some of the hydrogen peroxide had run into the landing skid well and collected there. Most of it had blown away when Zimmermann had extended the skid, but when he touched down there was still a little left. As the skid's shock absorbers took the force of the landing a small quantity of hydraulic oil was sprayed on to the hydrogen peroxide; and the reaction of the two chemicals caused the explosion. Once the cause was discovered, Me 163 pilots were warned to extend their landing skid immediately after pulling the hydrogen peroxide jettison handle, to allow the airflow as long as possible to blow away any of the chemical which collected on the skid.

During the day's fighting the Me 163s had been able to destroy four enemy bombers in return for one rocket fighter, Eisenmann's, damaged in combat and another, Zimmermann's, damaged on landing. After all that had gone before, I./JG 400 had achieved its first successes; yet the rocket fighter's victory score on this day was never to be equalled in the future.

September saw operations by JG 400 on five occasions, on the 10th, 11th, 12th, 13th and 28th. The strength of the unit's reaction

varied, with nine Me 163s being sent up on the last of these missions. But on all of them there were problems with ground control, and only a small proportion of the rocket fighters were able to intercept. For example, on the 28th Zimmermann was scrambled to engage an American formation flying past Brandis. Since he was to intercept at close to the limit of the Me 163's radius of action, to conserve fuel he did not use full throttle and took his aircraft up at a shallow angle of climb (for the Me 163, that is):

'Four minutes after take-off I sighted the B-17s, about 45 aircraft at about 10 o'clock at 7,700 m (25,000 ft). I myself was flying level at 9,200 m (30,000 ft) at about 800 kph (500 mph), in an excellent position. But about 1.5 km behind the formation my motor shut down, my fuel was exhausted. In a flat dive I curved round to the left on to the last B-17 in the box, and at 500 m I fired one burst without visible result.'

Lacking power, Zimmermann's Messerschmitt now began to fall behind the bombers. So in a final desperate attempt he pushed down the nose of his fighter to gain a little more speed, then pulled up for a snap attack from below on the same B-17 — only to have his guns jam at the critical moment. Seething with frustration, the German pilot broke away and began his long glide back to Brandis.

On 24 September JG 400 was listed as having 19 Me 163s on strength, of which 11 were available for operations. Since well over 100 Me 163Bs had been produced by this time it is clear that, as in the case of other German jet types, only relatively few of those built were reaching the front-line units.

Also during September, the rocket fighter programme suffered a crippling setback. Following Allied bombing attacks on Leverkusen and Ludwigshaven, where the IG Farbenindustrie plants produced most of the hydrazine hydrate in Germany, there was a severe cutback in the production of this important rocket fuel. The resultant shortages were to dog the Me 163 programme for the remainder of the war (a major competitor for the limited supplies was the V1 flying bomb, which required hydrazine hydrate to power its launching catapult).

During October there were further sporadic actions by the rocket fighters. After an

---

[1]Later production Me 163Bs were fitted with a system for jettisoning *T-Stoff*.

unsuccessful attempt to engage American bombers on the 5th, they were more successful on the 7th. Five Me 163s took off in the first wave and, before the escorting P-51s could do anything about it, *Feldwebel* Siegfried Schubert had shot down a B-17 of the 95th Bomb Group. Landing back at Brandis, Schubert strapped into another Me 163 to have a second crack at the B-17s. Then, in the words of Rudolf Zimmermann who watched the incident:

'He started, rolling faster and faster. Near the end of the grass runway he veered towards the left; something was wrong with his take-off dolley. He hit the grass at take-off speed, flipped over as if his left wheel had come off, then there was an explosion and everything was hidden in a large mushroom cloud. Our good friend Siegfried Schubert was no more.'

Though shaken at seeing one of their comrades meet such a violent end, the Me 163 pilots continued taking off in ones and twos to engage the enemy bombers. Zimmermann continued:

'*Leutnant* Bott and I took off at 1230 pm westbound, turning left and heading for the area 50 km south-east of Leipzig. Climbing, we opened out and began searching for targets. Looking down from an altitude of 11,000 m (36,000 ft), climbing at an angle of about 60 degrees at a speed of about 930 kph (580 mph) I saw below my right wing a lone B-17 at about 7,400 m (24,000 ft). Being above, I turned away circling to the left, the B-17 now being at about 1 o'clock and below, 1.5 km away. Then my motor shut down, indicating that my fuel was exhausted. I dived into a firing position, fired a burst and saw pieces flying off the bomber.'

Zimmermann's speed began to fall away, so he broke off and turned in the general direction of Brandis. A long way from base and over almost solid cloud cover, he was about to call for a homing when:

'At that moment the roof fell in. My aircraft was hit in the fuselage and on the left wing. About 80 m off my left wing a Mustang was overshooting me, his auxiliary tanks still in position. I myself was going at about 240 kph (150 mph), pulling in a steep turn to the left to get behind him. At that moment his No. 2 overshot me to the right. I continued turning and, getting head-on with his No. 3, I pressed my firing button. But in the sharp turn my guns jammed.'

Leading the Mustangs was Lieutenant Elmer Taylor of the 364th Fighter Group. As he overshot, Zimmermann pushed down the nose of his small fighter until he was diving almost vertically; his speed built up rapidly. Below him was almost complete cloud cover, except for a single hole through which he could see a reasonably sized field surrounded by trees. The German pilot continued:

'Soon out-diving the Mustangs in the opposite direction, I was ahead of the game, going down at about 880 kph (550 mph) and circling the meadow. Then, on approaching to land, my left wing fell as the speed dropped: the plywood skinning on the underside had been torn off by their bullets and the subsequent dive. I skimmed over the tree tops, chopping Christmas trees; my left wing dug into the ground, cutting short my landing run. I came to a halt in the middle of the field. Hearing the Mustangs approaching, I jumped out. As the first came in to attack I ran off at right angles, then dropped down. During several strafing runs my aircraft was shot up like a sieve.'

Despite the bullets flying all around him, the greatest danger to Zimmermann came from a 'friendly' Flak battery nearby; its gunners opened up enthusiastically at the low-flying Mustangs, sending several rounds which burst uncomfortably close to him.

After the Mustangs had broken off their attack and turned away for home. Zimmermann returned to his wrecked aircraft to survey the damage. It was then that he was surprised to see his friend *Feldwebel* Herbert Straznicky, who had taken off shortly before him in an Me 163, come walking towards him; how had Straznicky been able to reach the crash site so soon? Straznicky explained that he too had been pursued by Mustangs and had descended through the same hole in the clouds, but his Me 163 had come to rest almost up against the trees. While the Mustangs had strafed Zimmermann's aircraft, Straznicky had hidden in the trees and, when the attack ended, he returned to his Me 163 to find it untouched: his first thought was that the American pilots must have been lousy shots! Then he caught sight of Zimmermann's wrecked aircraft and the truth became clear. Straznicky's undamaged fighter was later collected and taken back to Brandis; Zimmermann's was a write-off.

Zimmermann and Straznicky had escaped unscathed, but in the meantime disaster had

Captain Fred Glover, flying a P-51 of the 4th Fighter Group, shot down *Oberfeldwebel* Guenther Andreas's Me 163 during the action on 2 November. The German pilot parachuted to safety. *Glover via Hess*

Feldwebel Rudolf Zimmermann's Me 163 photographed from Lieutenant Willard Erkamp's P-51, during the action on 7 October. The German pilot crash landed his damaged aircraft and was able to run safely clear, before strafing Mustangs wrecked the Messerschmitt on the ground. *USAF*

struck again at Brandis. *Unteroffizier* Manfred Eisenmann, returning in an aircraft that had probably suffered battle damage, side-slipped out of control during his landing approach. *Unteroffizier* Rudolf Glogner, sitting in a fully tanked rocket fighter awaiting the order to scramble, watched horrified as Eisenmann's Me 163 lurched in his direction. The aircraft struck the ground hard, rebounded into the air, then dropped one wing and tumbled across the grass breaking up as it careered past Glogner's and other waiting rocket fighters. Crash crews found Eisenmann's body still strapped inside what was left of the cabin.

Leutnant Hans Bott had damaged one B-17, and Siegfried Schubert had destroyed another before his fatal attempt at a second mission. But these victories had been soured by the loss of three Me 163s and two pilots killed on 7 October.

For the remainder of October there was little activity by JG 400, mainly due to the poor weather and the fuel shortage that was now beginning to bite. But on 2 November there was a powerful response to a heavy attack on Leuna by B-17s of the 3rd Air Division. *Leutnant* Hans Bott, *Oberfeldwebel* Jacob Bollenrath, *Oberfeldwebel* Guenther Andreas, Straznicky and Glogner took off and were accurately vectored into the vicinity of the enemy

bombers. Andreas was first into the attack, but his Me 163 immediately came under accurate return fire and a splinter hit him above the right eye. His aircraft crippled, he tried to bale out of the falling Messerschmitt, but his canopy refused to budge at first. The German pilot undid his seat harness and pushed against the plexiglass with all of his strength until, finally and to his great relief, it came away. Meanwhile, however, the escorting Mustangs had been closing in on the gliding rocket fighter. Captain Fred Glover, who was leading the 4th Fighter Group that day, afterwards reported:

'The aircraft made a 180 degree starboard turn and headed back east in a slight dive. I dropped my tanks and headed for it on a converging course. The aircraft headed east and myself north. As the enemy aircraft crossed in front of me I recognized it to be an Me 163 rocket ship. I made a quick 90 degree turn to the east and dropped in line astern. I opened fire immediately from a range of about 400 yards. I got immediate strikes on the tail, wings and cockpit. The belly of the Me 163 caught fire and exploded. Pieces came back and I closed rapidly, after the explosion. I overshot and laid my wing down to look at him. His tail was shot off and his canopy shot up badly [in fact, Andreas had released it by this time]. The Me 163 started to wallow and spin down still on fire.'

Andreas had not been aware of the presence of his assailant until the latter's rounds began striking his aircraft; throughout the attack he sat huddled in his seat not daring to move. Then, unscathed, he baled out of the stricken aircraft.

Andreas had had a very lucky escape but *Oberfeldwebel* Jacob Bollenrath, who attacked after him, was not so fortunate. Captain Louis Norley, also of the 4th Fighter Group, caught sight of Bollenrath running in to attack the bombers:

'We were just completing a port orbit waiting for the jets to come down when one did pop out at 6 o'clock to me. I immediately dropped my tanks, advancing full boost and revs. I set my gyro sight for 30 feet [wingspan of enemy aircraft] and closed the graticule to maximum range. I encountered no difficulty in putting the dot on the jet; however I was quite a little out of range — about 1,000 yards. I got on the jet's tail and followed him down. The jet started pulling away from me, so I fired a few short bursts hoping to make him turn whereby I could possibly cut him off and get in range. The jet did start to level out and make a port turn — his

Me 163 pilots of Jagdgeschwader 400, photographed at Brandis late in 1944: from left to right, Schorsch Neher, unidentified, Kristoph Kurz, and Jupp Muehlstroh. Note the two pilots in the background, wearing the special protective suits issued to rocket pilots. *Glogner*

speed dropped off considerably as his turn increased. I closed in very rapidly. I was using the K-14 sight for the first time and do not remember opening the graticule as I closed in; however I did get a couple of strikes on his tail, firing from 280 to 50 yards, 10° off. My speed was approximately 450 when I got into range. I throttled back but was unable to stay in the turn with him due to my excessive speed. I overshot him, pulled up and got on his tail again. Up to this time the jet had not been using his blower, at least he was not emitting any black smoke. As I closed on him the second time he used his blower for a couple of seconds and then cut it off again. I closed to 400 yards from 20° off, fired again and saw strikes on the tail. The jet rolled over, started straight down from 8,000 feet with fire coming intermittently from his port side and exhaust. He crashed in a small village and exploded.

Bollenrath was still inside the cockpit when his Me 163 hit the ground.

Meanwhile other Me 163s were closing in on the B-17s and the 91st, 94th, 388th, 452nd and 493rd Bomb Groups all reported encounters with them, though the attacks were not pressed home vigorously. None of the heavy bombers was hit by the rocket fighters and, although several American gunners reported engaging the Me 163s as they came within range, nobody claimed the destruction of any of them. There is reason to believe, however, that the return fire may have caused the destruction of *Feldwebel* Herbert Straznicky's Messerschmitt which plunged into the ground with the pilot still on board. With the loss of *Oberfeldwebel* Horst Rolly, killed during the

action, it had been another black day for I./JG 400: four Me 163s destroyed and three pilots killed, but no enemy aircraft shot down.

Small though it was, the engagement on 2 November was to be the last on such a scale by I./JG 400 for more than four months. The continual shortages of rocket fuel and trained pilots, together with the poor weather during the final winter of the war, combined to reduce Me 163 operations to a negligible level. In such a climate of difficulty the formation of a second *Gruppe* of Me 163s, II./JG 400 based at Stargad in Pomerania, added little to the operational effectiveness of the type. On 10 January 1945 I./JG 400, the only unit then operational, had 46 rocket fighters on its strength of which 16 were recorded as being serviceable; II./JG 400 probably had a similar number. Production of the Me 163 came to an end in February 1945, after about 364 had been built.

Me 163 attacking an enemy bomber using *Jaegerfaust*, upwards firing guns triggered automatically by a photoelectric cell as it passed underneath. For each 50 mm shell fired upwards, an equivalent counterweight was fired downwards to balance out the recoil.

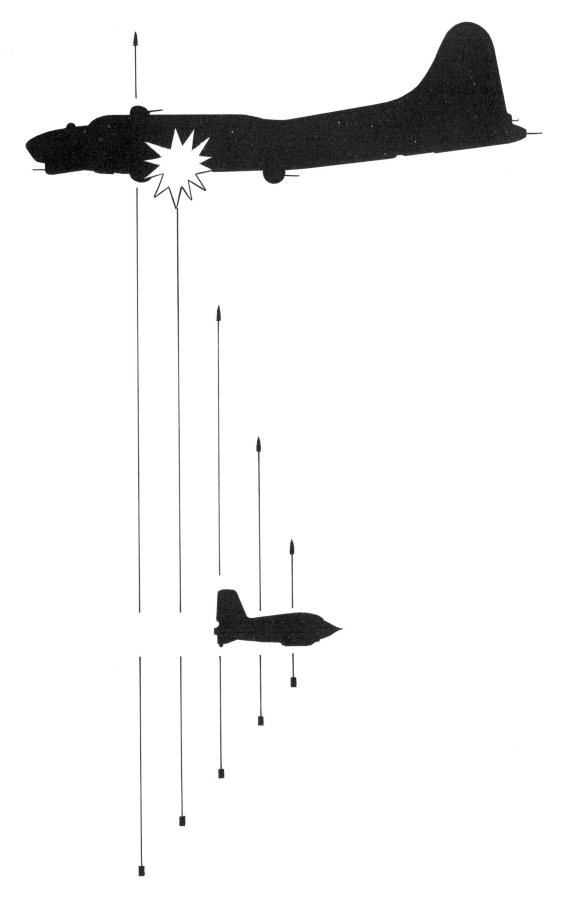

In March 1945 there was a resurgence of activity by JG 400, culminating with five sorties on the 15th; none of the rocket fighters succeeded in getting through to the bombers on that day, however, and one Me 163 was claimed by an escorting Mustang.

One of the factors that had prevented the Me 163 from becoming an effective bomber-destroyer was the lack of an armament system which enabled any but the most skilful of pilots to deliver an accurate and destructive burst during the brief attacking runs. Closing in on their targets at an overtaking speed of about 150 m (160 yards) per second, many pilots found that by the time they had their sight on a bomber it was time to break away to avoid colliding with it. To overcome this problem the Hasag company in Leipzig developed *Jaegerfaust* ('fighter-fist'), an automatic firing system. As applied to the Me 163, *Jaegerfaust* comprised ten vertically mounted 50 mm gun barrels built into the wing roots, five on each side. Each barrel was loaded with a single 1 kg (2.2 pound) high explosive shell; to balance out the recoil forces, as the shells were fired *upwards* at the enemy aircraft, counterweights weighing as much as the shells were fired *downwards* and clear of the Me 163. The barrels were fired in rapid succession, triggered by a photo-electric cell which detected the shadow of the enemy aircraft as it passed overhead. All the Me 163 pilot had to do was to prime the *Jaegerfaust* and fly his aircraft underneath the target bomber within about 100 m (325 feet) either from tail-on or, if he wished, from head-on. The barrels were divided into two groups of five for firing, enabling the pilot to carry out two attacks before he had to land to reload.

Jaegerfaust would have enabled a poorly trained pilot to make accurate attacks on enemy bombers, and great things were expected from it. The system performed impressively during trials against a cloth target the size of a bomber's wing, stretched between two tethered ballons. Before the end of the war about a dozen Me 163s were modified to carry *Jaegerfaust*, but only once was it used in action. On 10 April 1945 *Leutnant* Fritz Kelb took off to test it out and caught a lone B-17 straggling behind its formation near Leipzig. He made a single devastating high speed attack with the new weapon and the American bomber went down shedding pieces.

Kelb's attack marked the virtual end of the Me 163's operational career. Sparkling though its speed and climb performance undoubtedly were, the aircraft operated too close to the limit of what was possible to have achieved much in war; it is doubtful whether, after almost a year in service, the rocket fighter caused the destruction of more than 16 enemy aircraft. The chemical rocket fuels were rather too exotic for general service use; and the bombing of just two key factories, coupled with the general chaos of the final six months of the war, crippled the production of one of the fuels, hydrazine hydrate. The jettisonable dolly undercarriage, which helped keep down the size and weight of the airframe, meant that the aircraft was difficult to move around prior to take-off, and after landing it was immobile until one of the specially-built lifting trolleys reached it. Once the fuel had been burnt the pilot was committed to landing the aircraft on his first attempt — the *T-Stoff* tank had to be empty prior to the landing, or there was the near-certainty of an explosion if there was a landing accident. During the Second World War, to be effective a fighting aircraft had to suffer fools gladly for training standards in all air forces fell far below those in peace time. The Me 163 forgave few mistakes and losses in accidents far exceeded those it inflicted on the enemy. Significantly, although each of the major Allied powers received captured Me 163s after the war, and the USA, USSR, Britain and France all later developed high performance rocket fighters of their own, nobody else has yet introduced the type into service. In retrospect it seems clear that the rocket fighter, for all its spectacular performance, is in fact a blind alley off the main path of fighter development.

Opposite: *Leutnant* **Fritz Kelb of JG 400, who scored the sole victory with the** *Jaegerfaust* **upwards firing weapon on 10 April 1945. He was killed just before the war ended.** *Glogner*

War's End

Glossary

Luftwaffe unit organisation

The basic operational unit for fighters, fighter-bombers, reconnaissance aircraft and bombers in the Luftwaffe was the *Gruppe*. This comprised three or four *Staffeln* each with an establishment of between nine and 16 aircraft, plus a staff (*Stab*) unit of three or four; thus a *Gruppe* had a strength of between 30 and 68 aircraft. During the closing stages of the war, however, actual unit strengths were often considerably below establishment.

A feature of the jet aircraft was that in many cases these were flown by ad hoc *Kommandos* (detachments) operating independently, whose strengths varied between a small *Staffel* and a *Gruppe*.

A *Geschwader* had a nominal strength of three or four *Gruppen* and the aircraft within it were usually assigned to a single role, for example *Jagdgeschwader* (abbreviated to JG), fighters; *Nachtjagd-* (NJG), night fighters and *Kampfgeschwader* (KG), bombers. Reconnaissance units were usually independent *Gruppen*, *Aufklaerungsgruppen* (Aufkl. Gr). It should be noted, however, that no *Geschwader* ever received its full establishment of jet aircraft.

The *Gruppen* within a *Geschwader* were numbered in Roman numerals before the *Geschwader* designation; thus the Third *Gruppe* of *Jagdgeschwader* 7 was abbreviated as III./JG 7. The *Staffeln* within a *Geschwader* were numbered consecutively using Arabic numerals. Thus in a unit of three *Gruppen* each of three *Staffeln*, the 1st, 2nd and 3rd *Staffeln* comprised the Ist *Gruppe*; the 4th, 5th and 6th *Staffeln* comprised the IInd *Gruppe* and the 7th, 8th and 9th *Staffeln* comprised the IIIrd *Gruppe*. The ninth *Staffel* of *Kampfgeschwader* 76 was therefore abbreviated to 9./KG 76, and was part of III./KG 76.

The basic *fighting* element in a Luftwaffe fighter unit was the *Rotte* or pair of aircraft; two *Rotten* made up a *Schwarm* of four aircraft and three or four *Schwaerme* comprised a *Staffel*. Sometimes the *Kette* of three aircraft was employed as the basic fighting element, for example by the Me 262s of the ad hoc fighter unit *Jagdverband 44* at the end of the war.

	Luftwaffe	Royal Air Force	USAAF
Equivalent Ranks	*Generalfeldmarschall*	Marshal of the RAF	General (five star)
	Generaloberst	Air Chief Marshal	General (four star)
	General	Air Marshal	Lieutenant General
	Generalleutnant	Air Vice Marshal	Major General
	Generalmajor	Air Commodore	Brigadier General
	Oberst	Group Captain	Colonel
	Oberstleutnant	Wing Commander	Lieutenant Colonel
	Major	Squadron Leader	Major
	Hauptmann	Flight Lieutenant	Captain
	Oberleutnant	Flying Officer	First Lieutenant
	Leutnant	Pilot Officer	Second Lieutenant
	Oberfaehnrich	Officer Cadet	Officer Cadet
	Feldwebel	Sergeant	Sergeant
	Unteroffizier	Corporal	Corporal
	Flieger	Aircraftman	Private

Bibliography

Eric Brown: *Wings of the Luftwaffe*, Macdonald and Janes

Jeffrey Ethell: *Komet*, Ian Allan

Roger Freeman: *The Mighty Eighth*, Macdonald and Janes

William Green: *Warplanes of the Third Reich*, Macdonald and Janes

William Green: *Rocket Fighter*, Ballantine

David Irving: The Rise and Fall of the Luftwaffe, Weidenfeld

Ernst Obermaier: *Die Ritterkreuzträger der Luftwaffe*, Hoffmann

Karl Pawlas: *Arado Ar 234, der erste Strahlbomber der Welt*, Luftfahrt

Alfred Price: *Battle over the Reich*, Ian Allan

Alfred Price: *World War II Fighter Conflict*, Macdonald and Janes

Hanfried Schliephake: *Flugzeugbewaffnung*, Motorbuch-Verlag

Chris Shores: *2nd TAF*, Osprey

J. Richard Smith and Anthony Kay: *German Aircraft of the Second World War*, Putnam

Mano Ziegler: *Turbinenjäger Me 262*, Motorbuch-Verlag

140

Index